First and foremost, I would like to give my heartfelt thank you to Helen for her on-going support of my photography pursuits.

Thank you to the organizers, Troy Hilton, Ben Vanlier and Richard Trotter along with the army of others that worked tirelessly to make this event as great as it was.

Thank you to all the bands for putting on such epic performances, thank you to Jill for helping me shape the book into it's final form and thank you to Lucia for the daily summaries and thank you to everyone else who contributed a piece of their memories (be it images or text) to populate the book with such awesome content. You are all awesome!

Looking forward to next year!

Adrian Onsen

I0472703

This photobook contains a small sample of photos from the festival. If you would like to see more photos, visit the websites of the photographers that contributed to this project.
Full photographer bios are at the back of the book.

AFTERMATH

Table of Contents

04   Introduction

Day 1 - Thursday
08   Peter Turns Pirate
10   Alter Der Ruine
12   Ego Likeness
14   FGFC820
16   William Control
18   The Dreaming
20   Bruderschaft
22   Leæther Strip

Day 2 - Friday
26   Dead on TV
28   Stoneburner
30   Kevorkian Death Cycle
32   Nitro/Noise
34   Mr.Kitty
36   Ludovico Technique
38   Tactical Sekt
40   Velvet Acid Christ

Day 3 - Saturday
46   Glenn Love
48   Electrovot
50   Mend
52   Squid Lid
54   GoFight
56   3TEETH
58   Conjure One
60   Haujobb

60   Reflections on the Festival

65   Epilogue

66   Photographer Bios

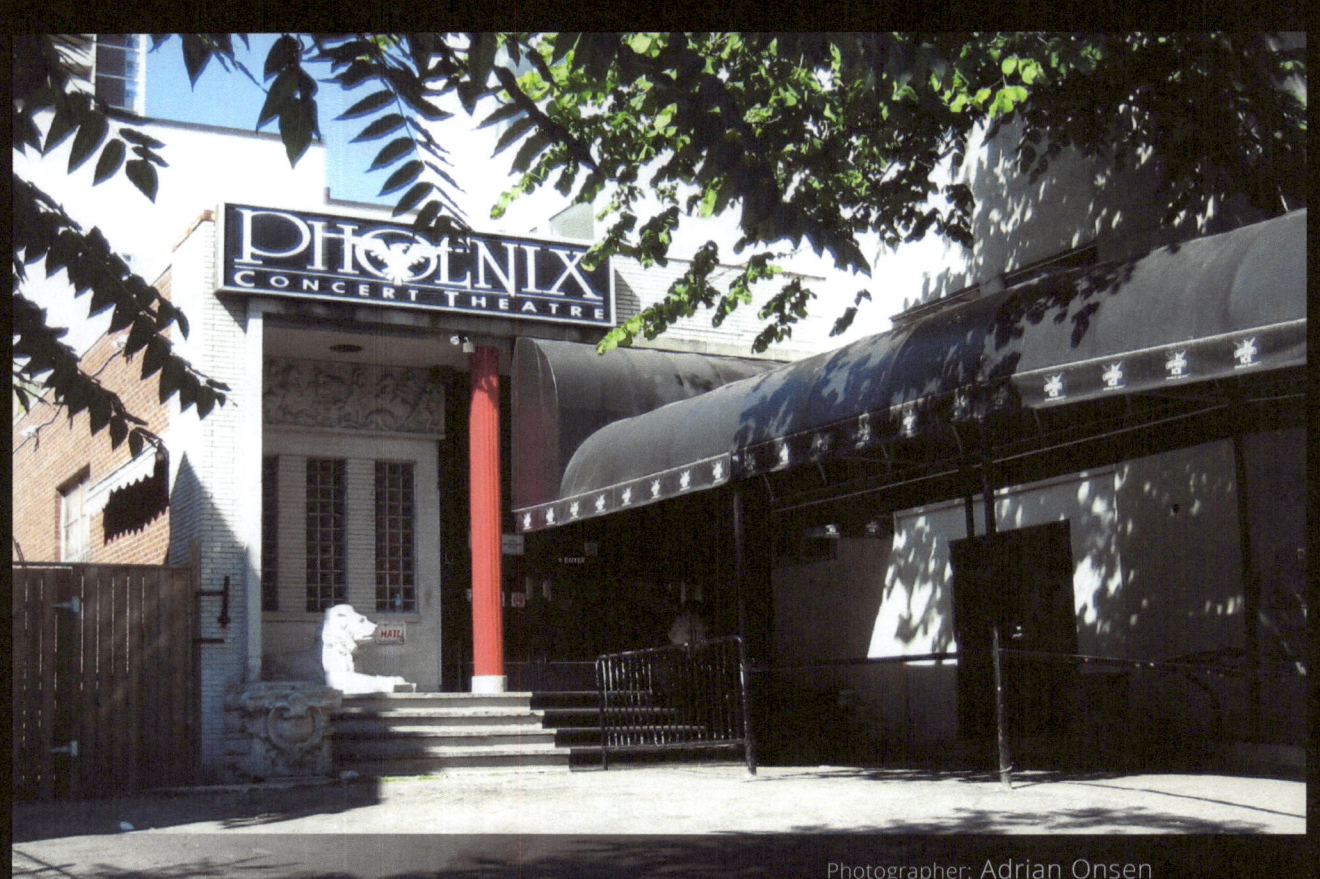

Photographer: Adrian Onsen

Introduction

Aftermath, to me, was exciting. The first one was different. It was a rescue operation. This year we had the opportunity to stand on our own two feet. I'm not going to say that it was easy, or perfect, but I'm proud of it. We had an amazing selection of artists, who gave their all in an amazing room with an amazing crew. To see all the smiling faces, from beginning to end was undescribable. The talent we got to work with are some of the most down to earth people in this scene. It was a wonderful experience. In order to make this happen, there are so many to thank.

First I want to thank my brothers in arms - Richard Trotter - you convinced me to do this again and put your balls on the line to ensure it happened. I can't thank you enough. I, and this scene owe you.

Ben Vanlier - without you, there'd be no heart or soul. The laughs and the talks helped keep me sane. Thank you.

My crew

Lisa Nadie - you've come a long way since we first met and I don't give you enough credit. Thank you for getting all the little shit done so I can focus on the big things.

Shane Scare, Richie Lentz, Paul Krieg, Mel Hutchinson, Jonathan Kaplan, Ethan Moseley, Ryan Cameron-Clark, Megan Trotter, Pat - you guys are the unsung heroes, making sure everything happened the way it should and to the standards I hold. Thank you.

Alison Cameron-Clark, Tasha Golden and Kym Britnell - thank you for the endless support, errands and understanding. Without you, this could not have happened.

Karen Stewart - Our lovely door girl. She misses the entire show, yet without her, there'd be no show. Thank you.

Vlad McNeally for the excellent website.

Tom and Christian at High Road Publicity for spreading the word and lining up all the awesome press.

The Phoenix Concert Theatre staff and security - they have supported us since day one when this was just an idea. This year they were swapping shifts just to be a part of this. They deserve all the credit in the world.

The bands and djs - You guys are the talent and every single one of you brought your A game. You fucking blew the roof off the place and breathed life into this thing. Thank you all from the bottom of my heart and we'll see you on the road, sometime, somewhere.

Finally, the crowd. This is about you guys. Always was and always will be. Every one of you who came out and showed support. Who spread the word. You are the scene. No one can every take that away from you no matter what they say.

Thank you all

Troy Hilton

AFTERMATH

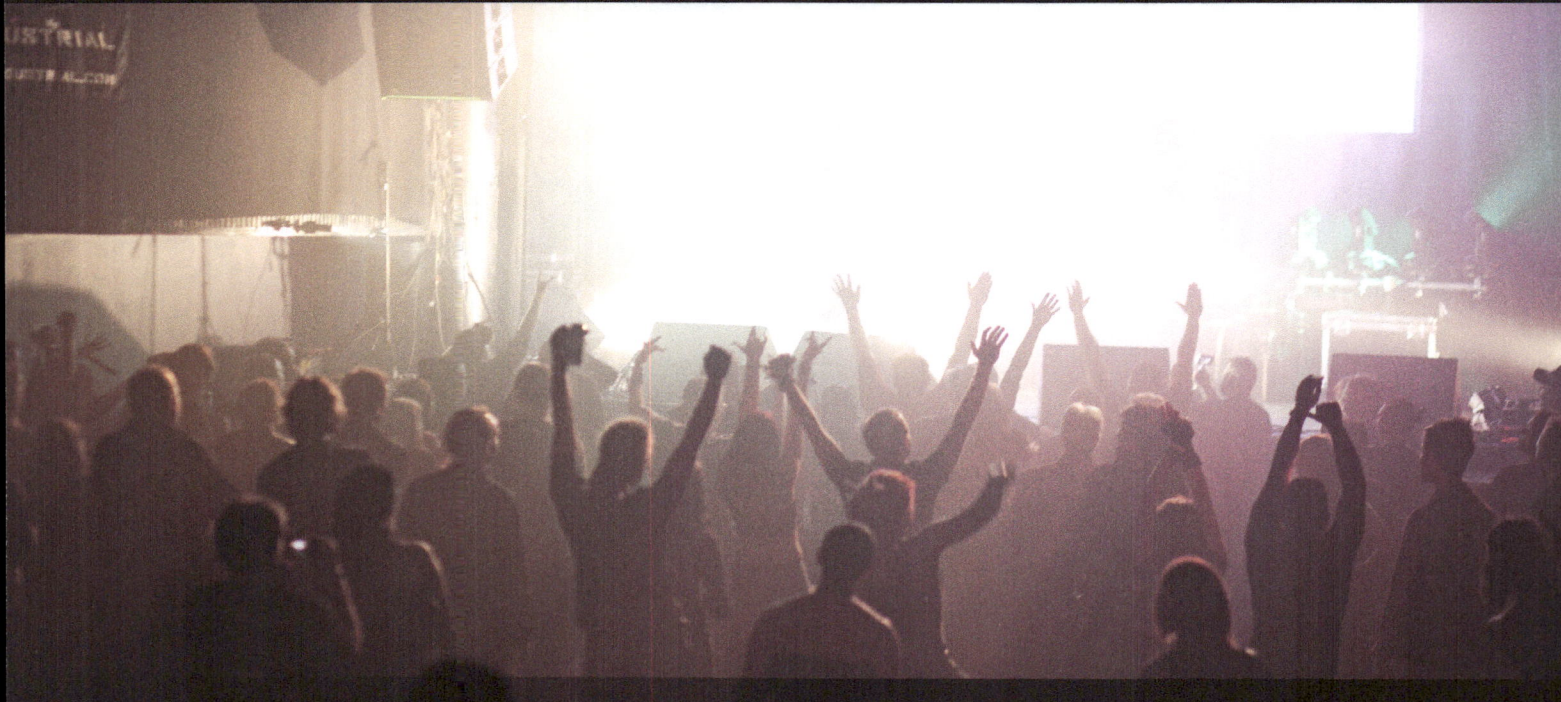

Day 1
Thursday, 27 August, 2015

The 2015 edition of Aftermath Festival featured an unprecedented variety of international talent.

Over the course of four days, no less than twenty-four artists and a dozen DJs took to the Phoenix Concert Theatre stage, delighting their audience with industrial, EBM, aggrotech and futurepop anthems.

The symbolism behind the venue's namesake is hardly lost on us: Aftermath sprung from the ashes of Kinetik Festival. Its second incarnation was electric - a triumphant return of Toronto's burgeoning legacy in the dark electronic music world.

Thursday evening, the excitement was palpable. A steady column of people had already formed outside the Phoenix doors; many had travelled far for the occasion. Animated conversations sprung up and friendships kindled as dark electronic music aficionados rejoiced in the opportunity to meet.

That is the lasting impact of festivals like Aftermath: they strengthen communities. They provide a venue for fans and artists alike to come together, to share their passions and to engage in fruitful collaborations.

We are tremendously grateful to the organizers, artists and disciples alike.

This is a tribute to all your dedication.

Peter Turns Pirate
Alter Der Ruine
Ego Likeness
FGFC820
Willam Control
The Dreaming
Bruderschaft
Leæther Strip

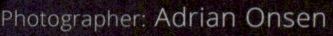

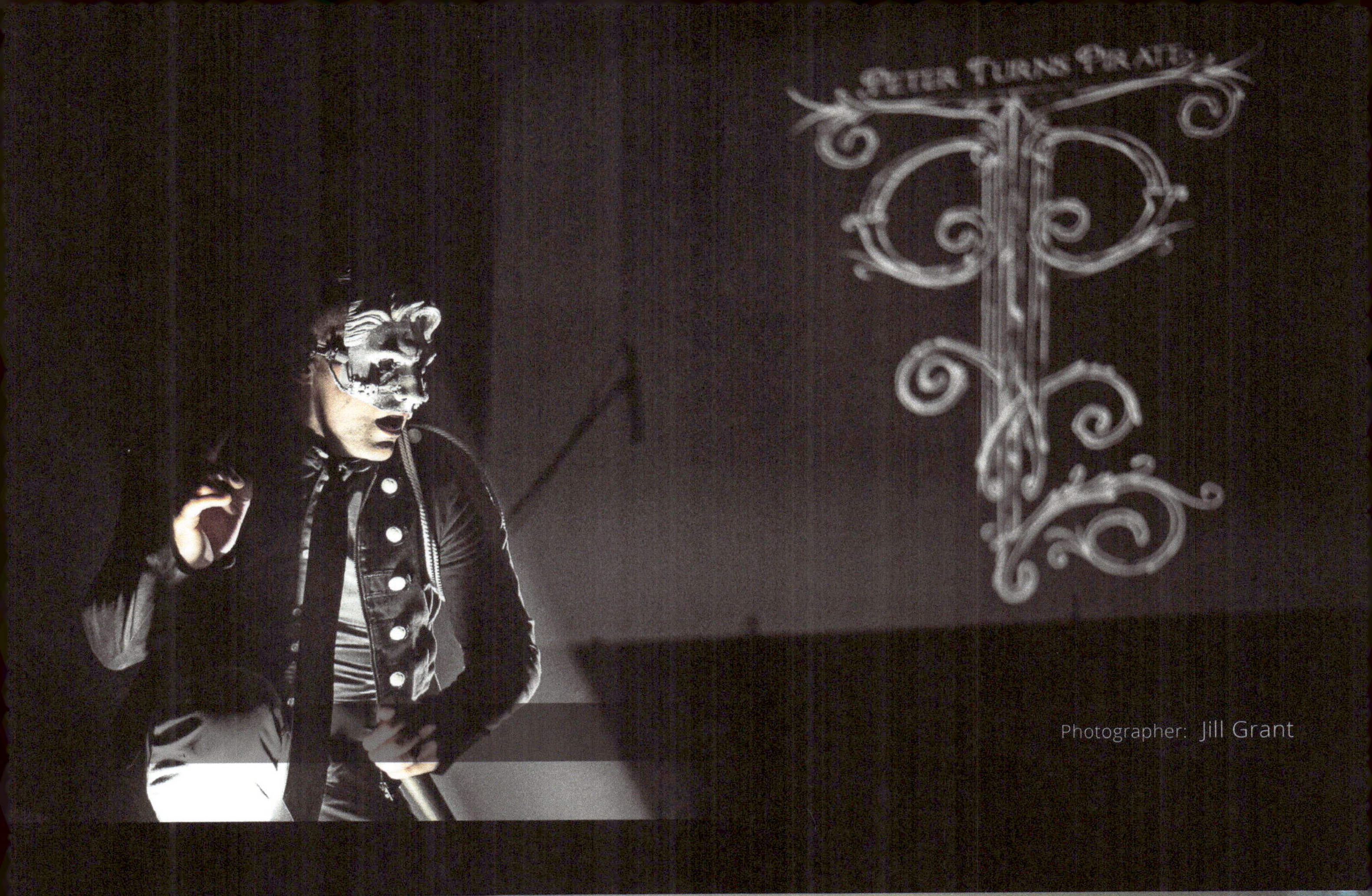

PETER TURNS PIRATE

Photographer: Jill Grant

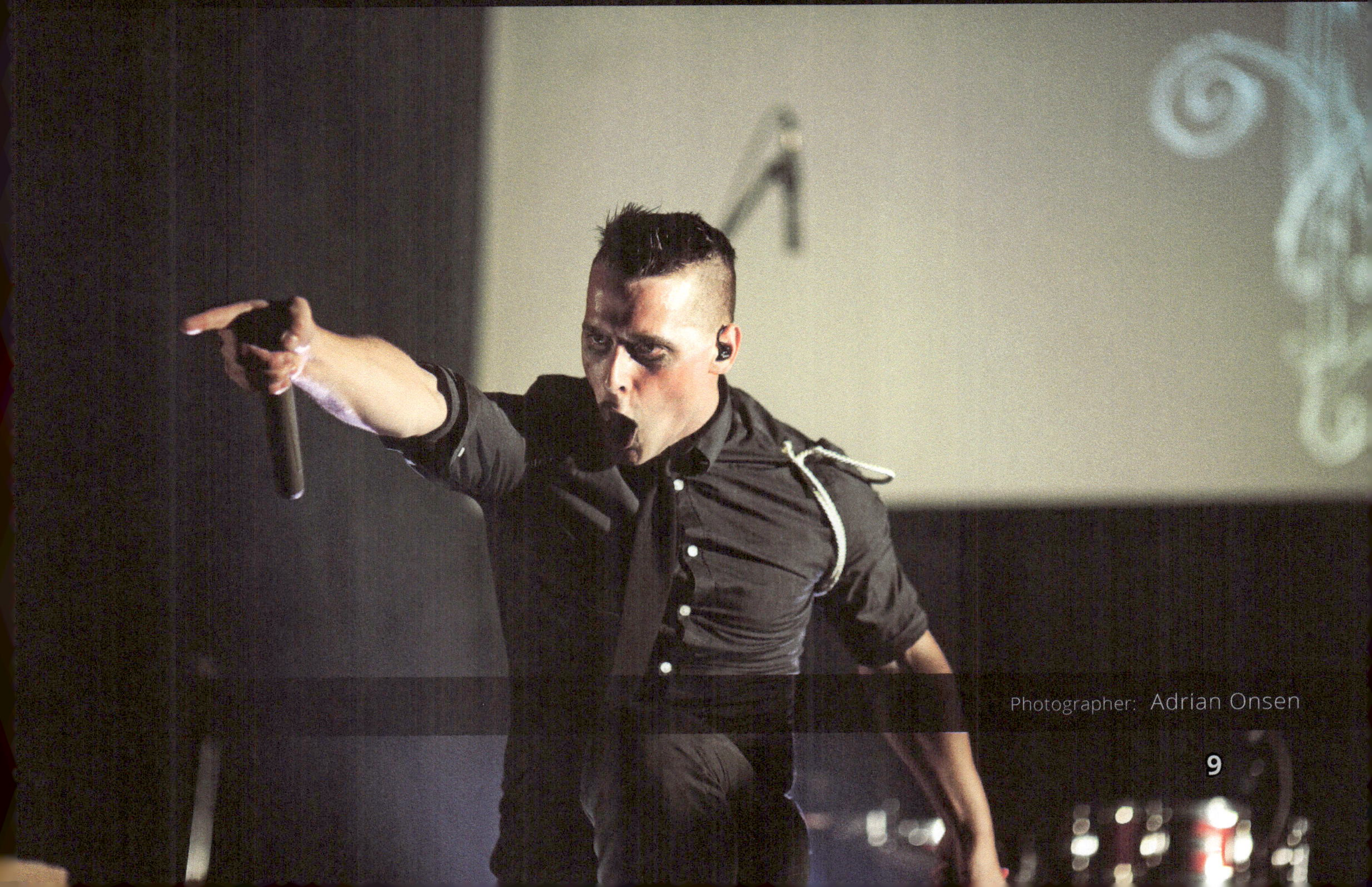

Photographer: Adrian Onsen

9

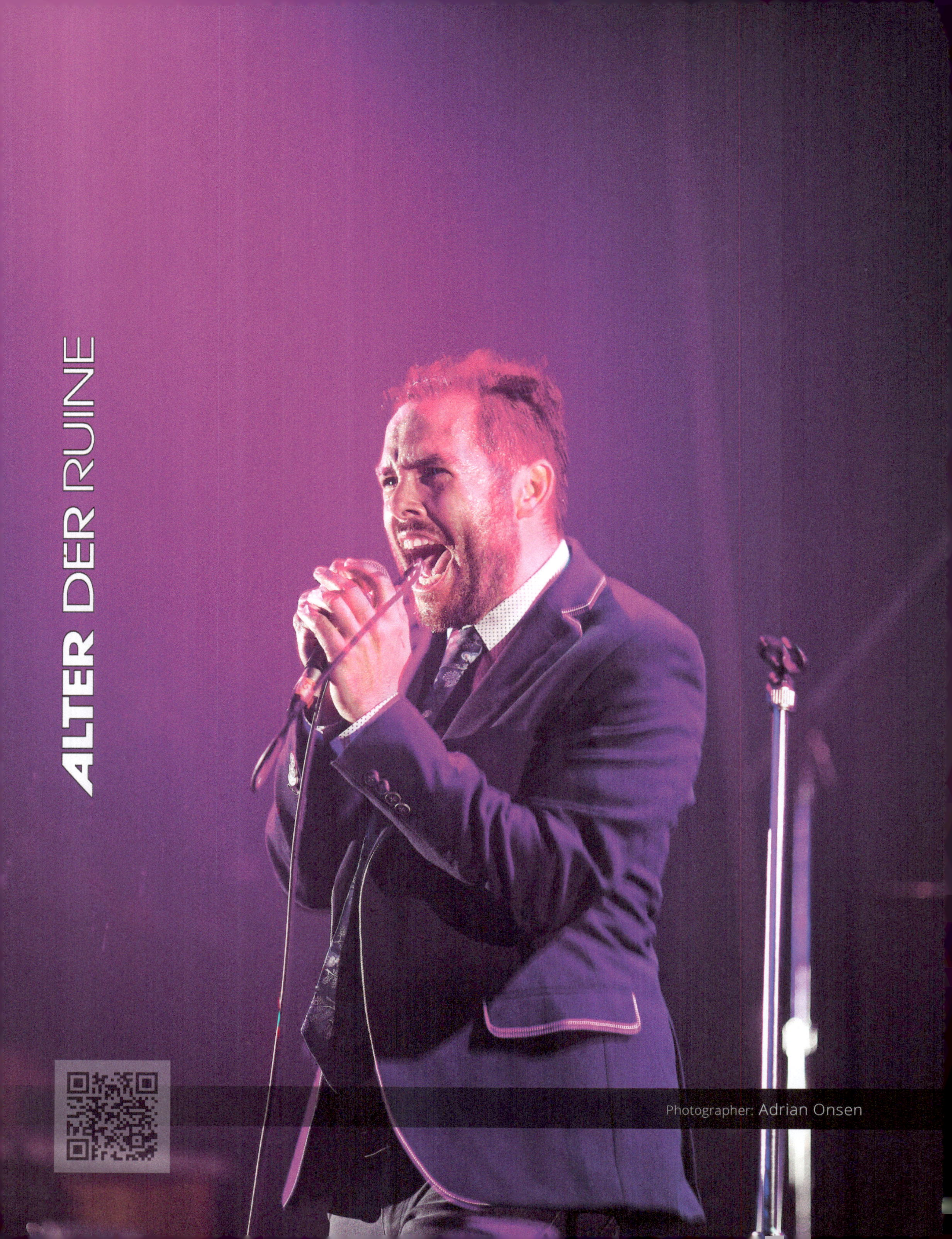

ALTER DER RUINE

Photographer: Adrian Onsen

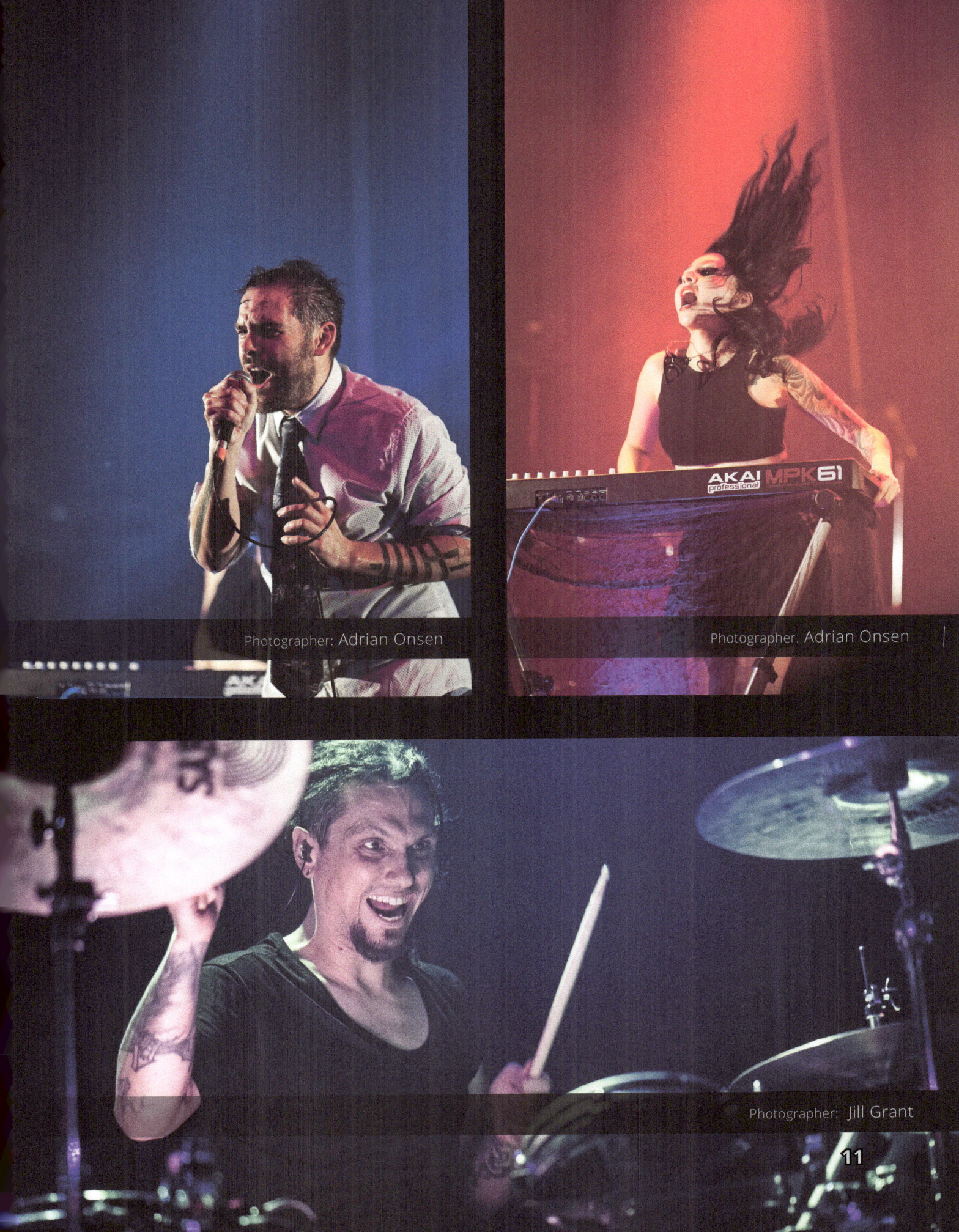

Photographer: Adrian Onsen

Photographer: Adrian Onsen

Photographer: Jill Grant

EGO LIKENESS

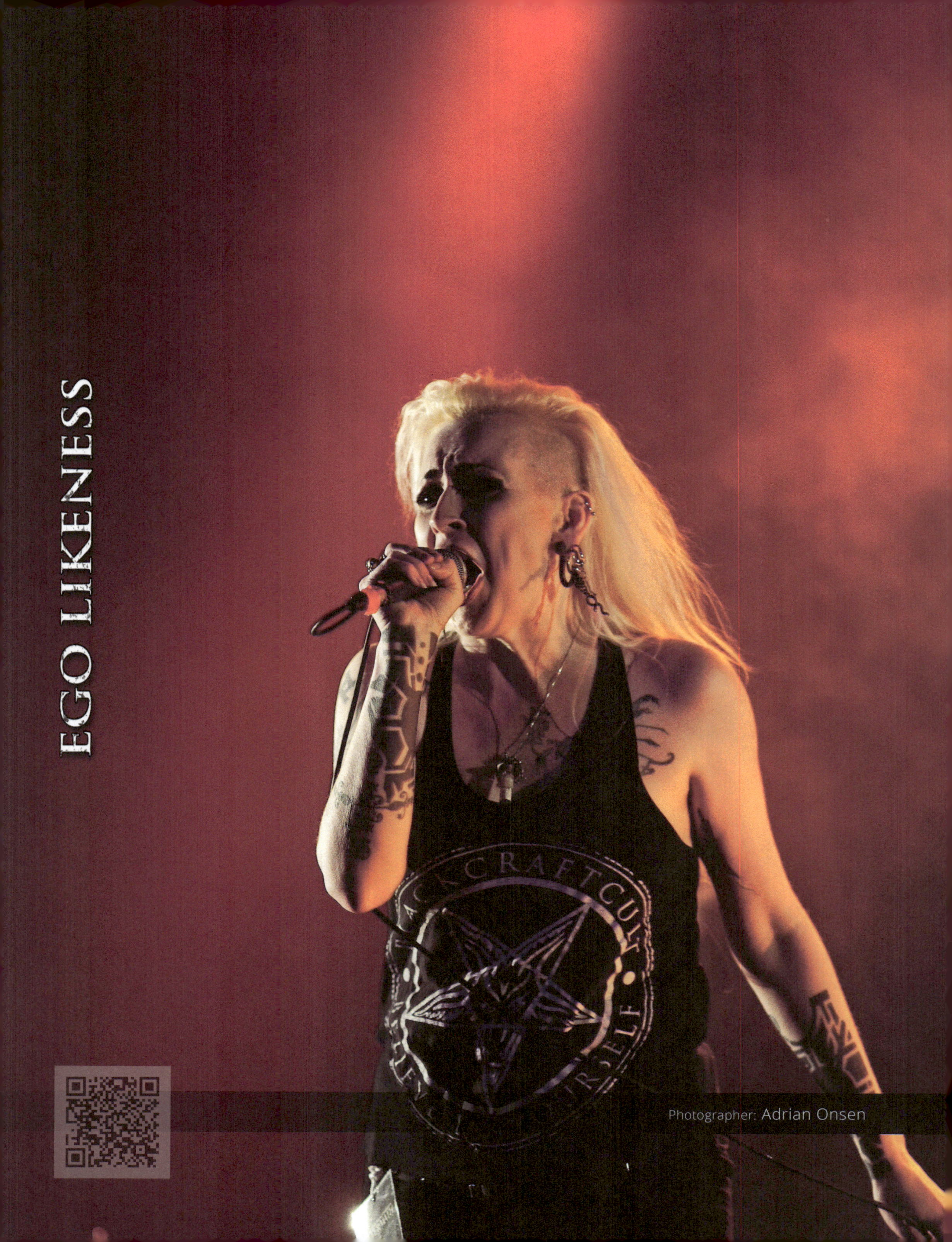

Photographer: Adrian Onsen

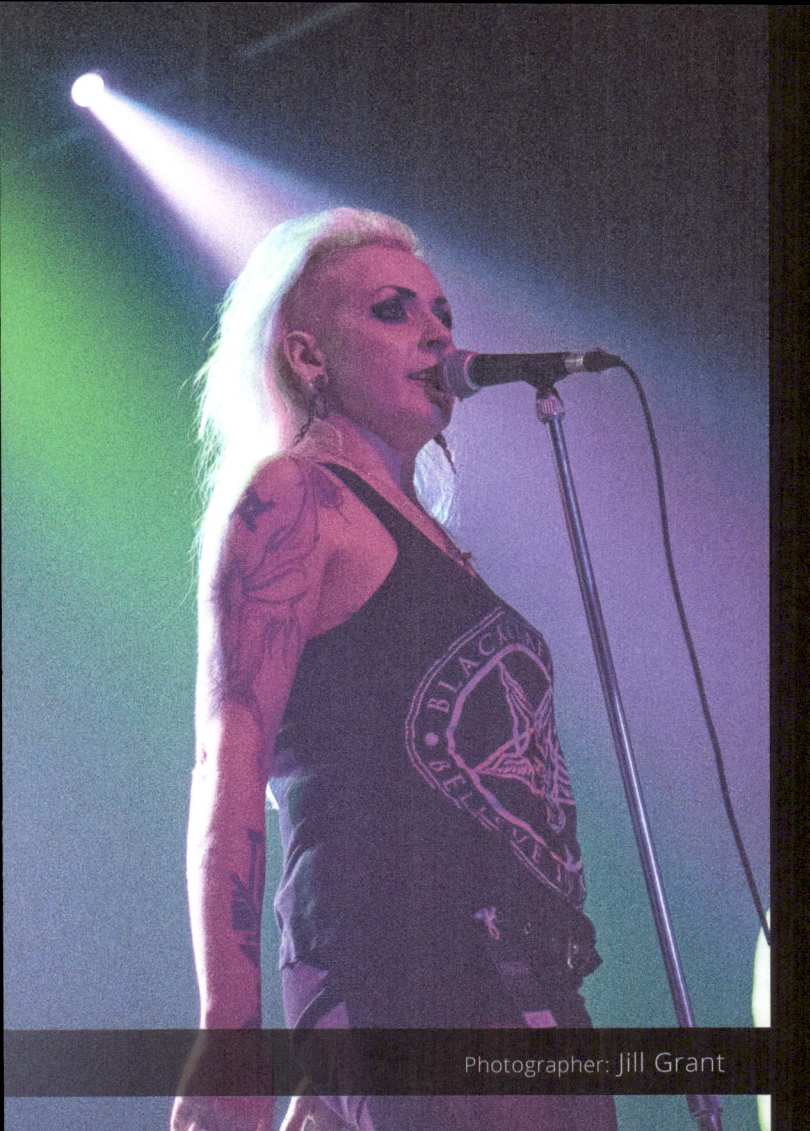

Photographer: Jill Grant

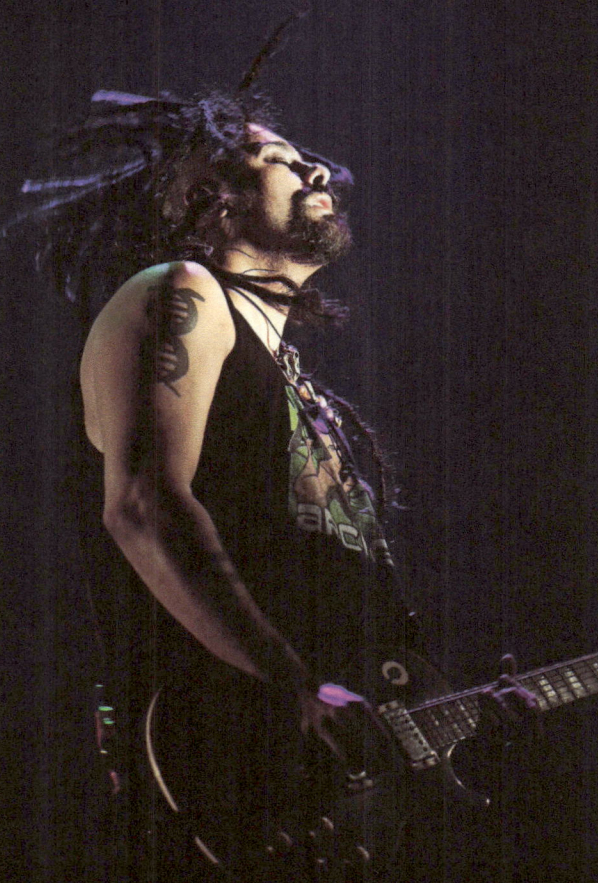

Photographer: Adrian Onsen

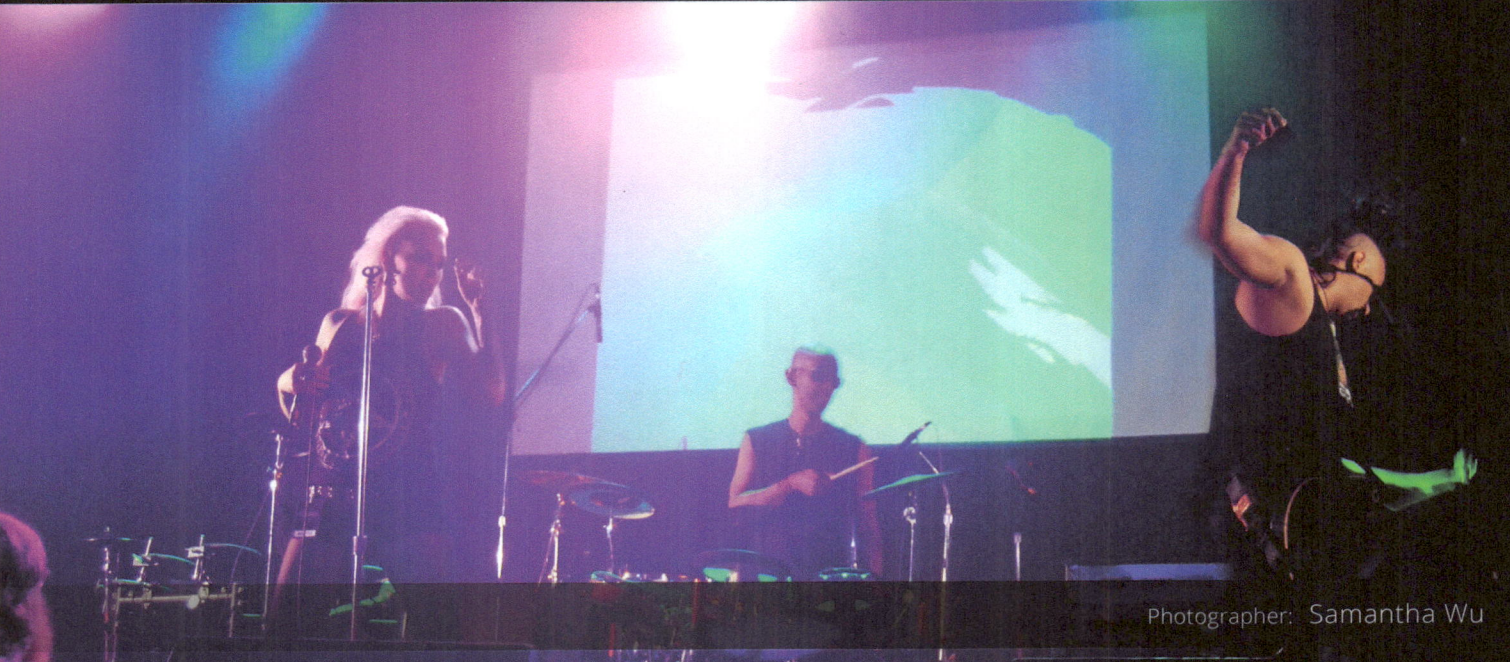

Photographer: Samantha Wu

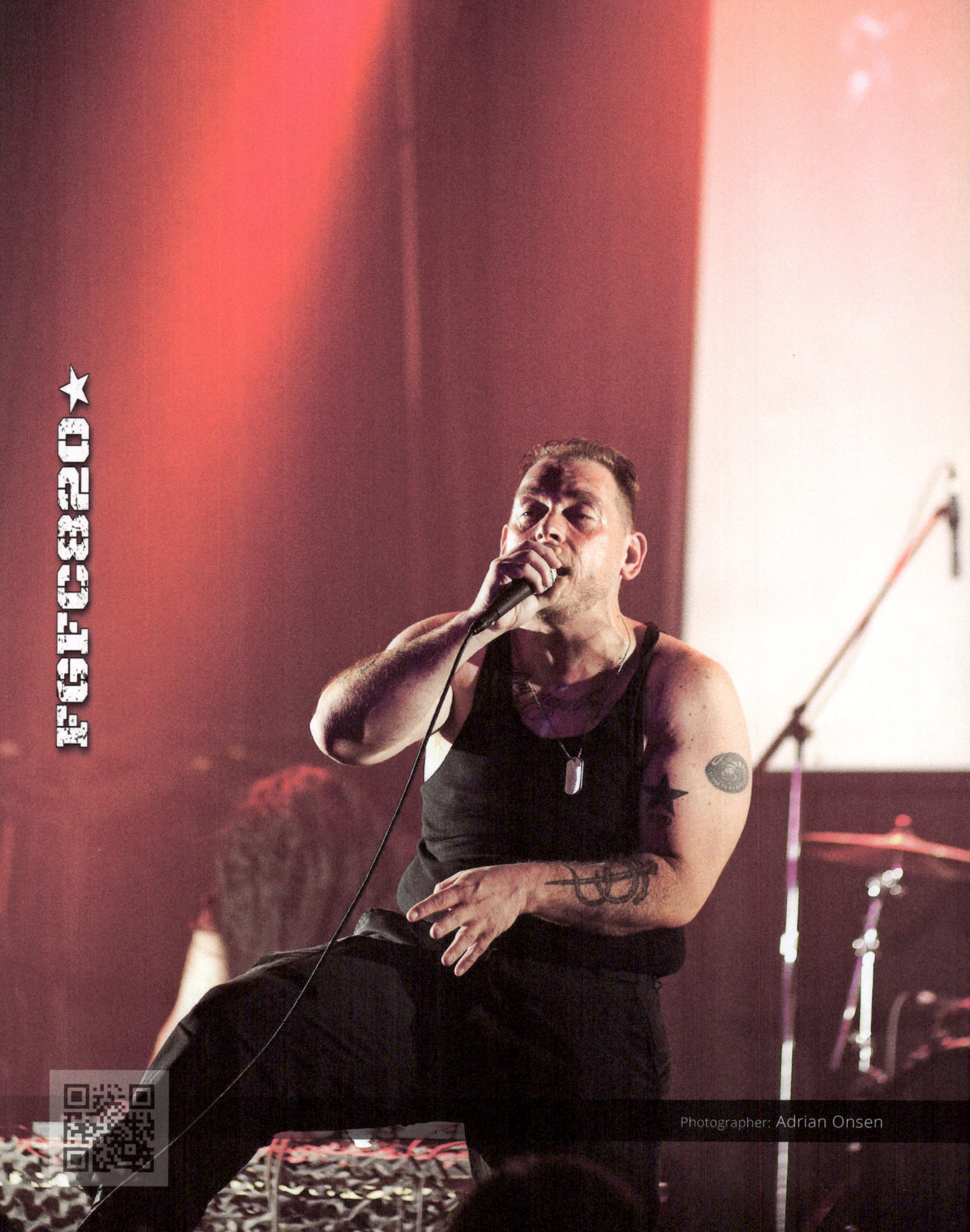

FGFC820★

Photographer: Adrian Onsen

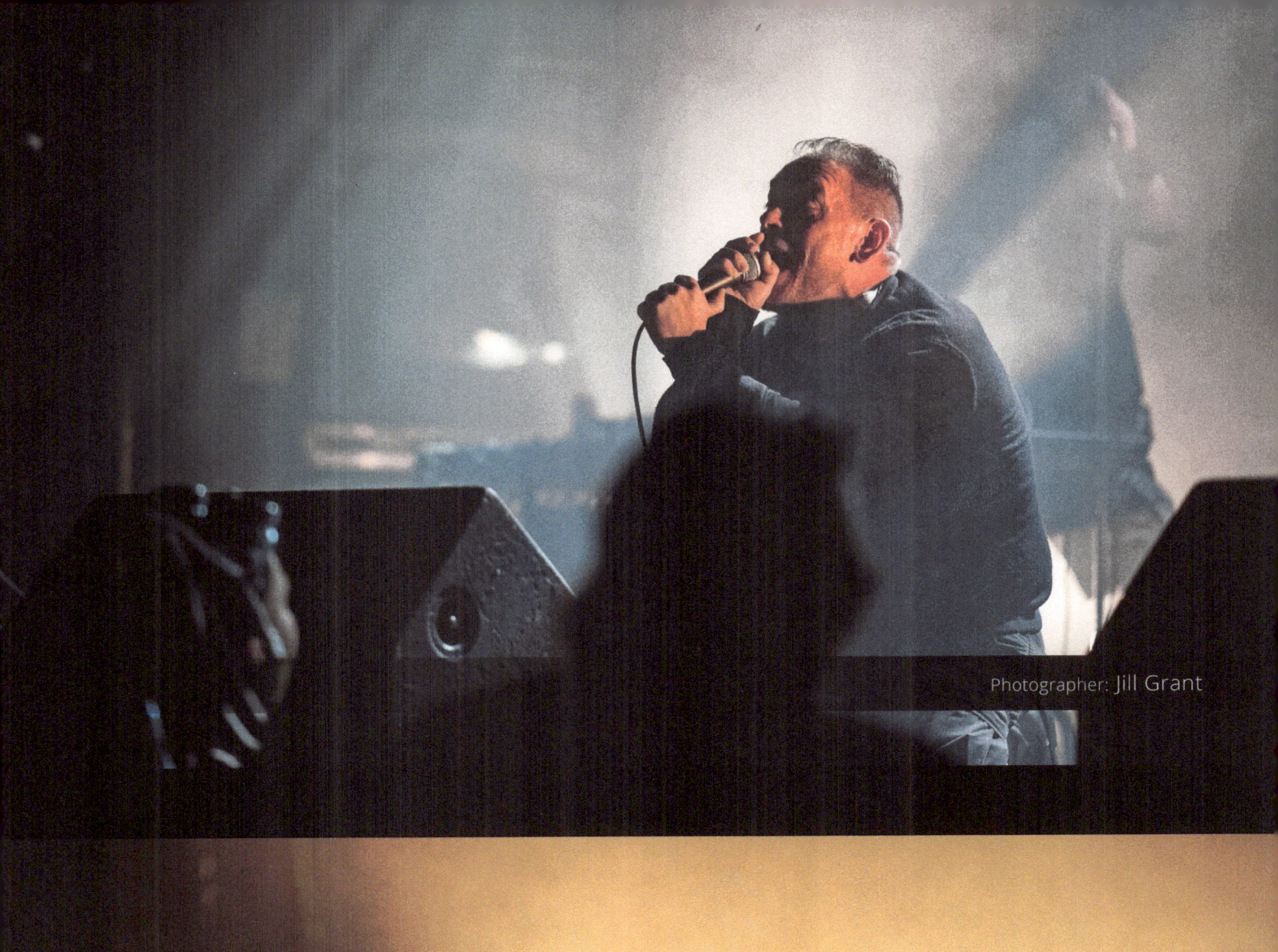

Photographer: Jill Grant

Photographer: Adrian Onsen

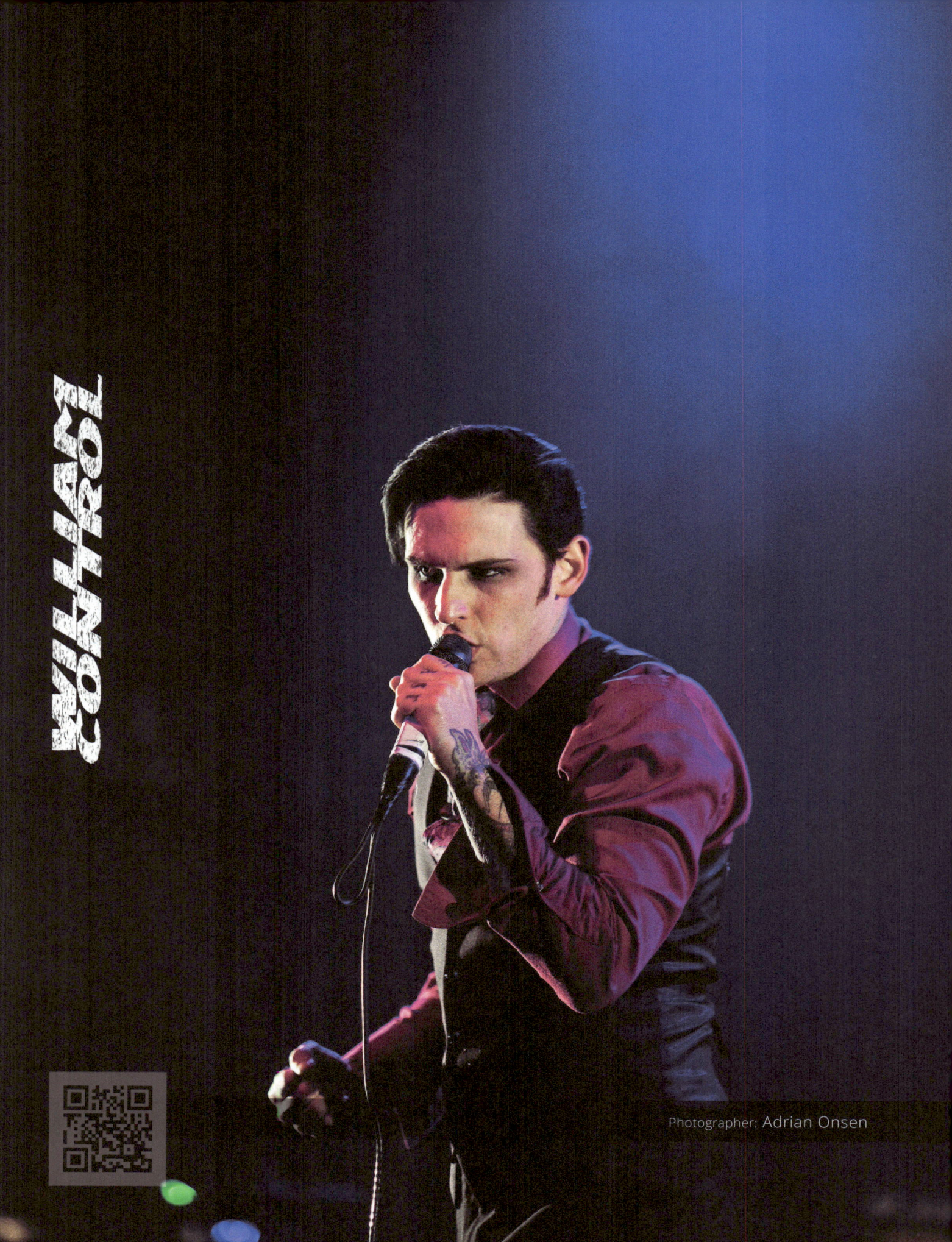

WILLIAM CONTROL

Photographer: Adrian Onsen

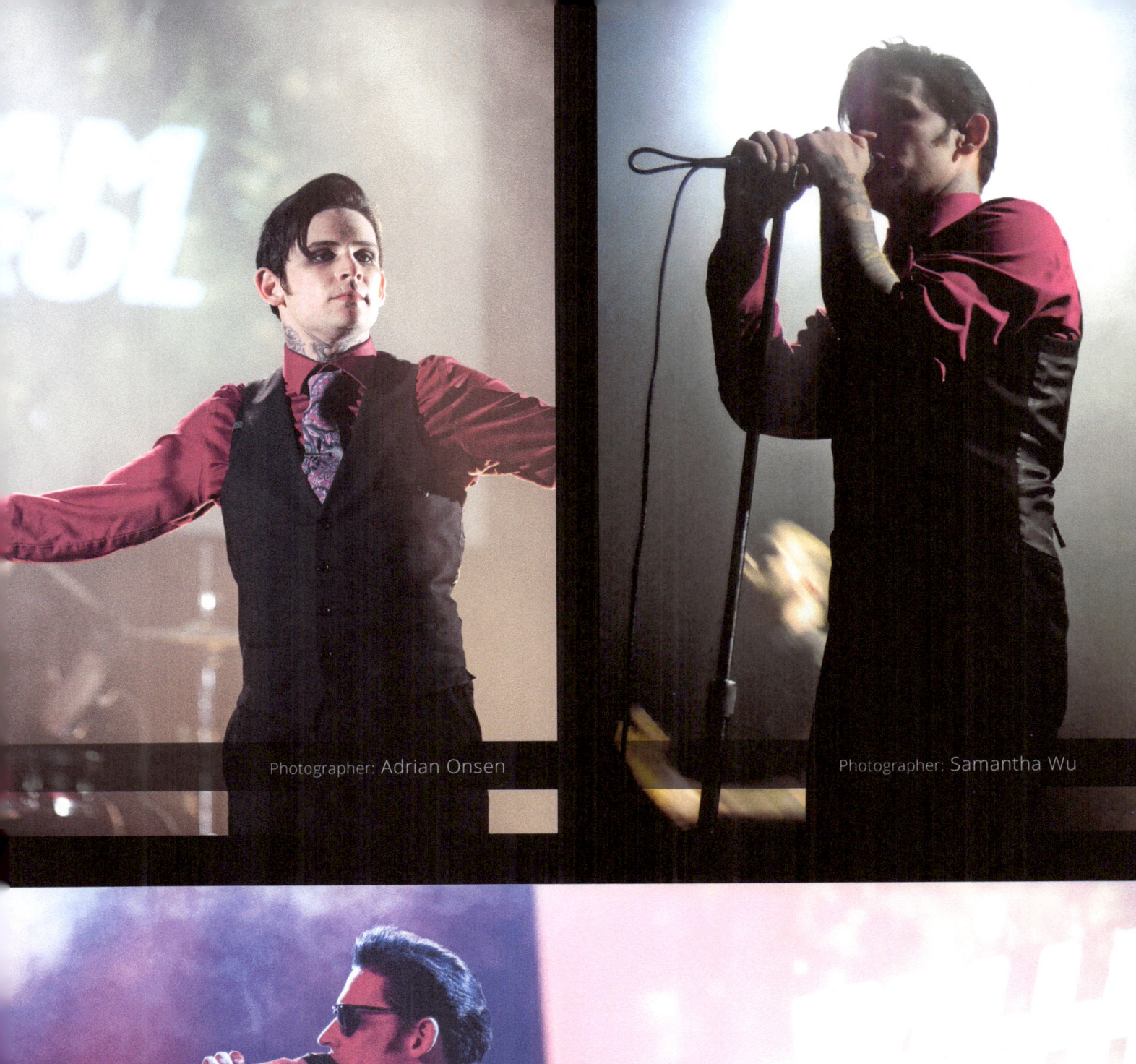

Photographer: Adrian Onsen

Photographer: Samantha Wu

Photographer: Jill Grant

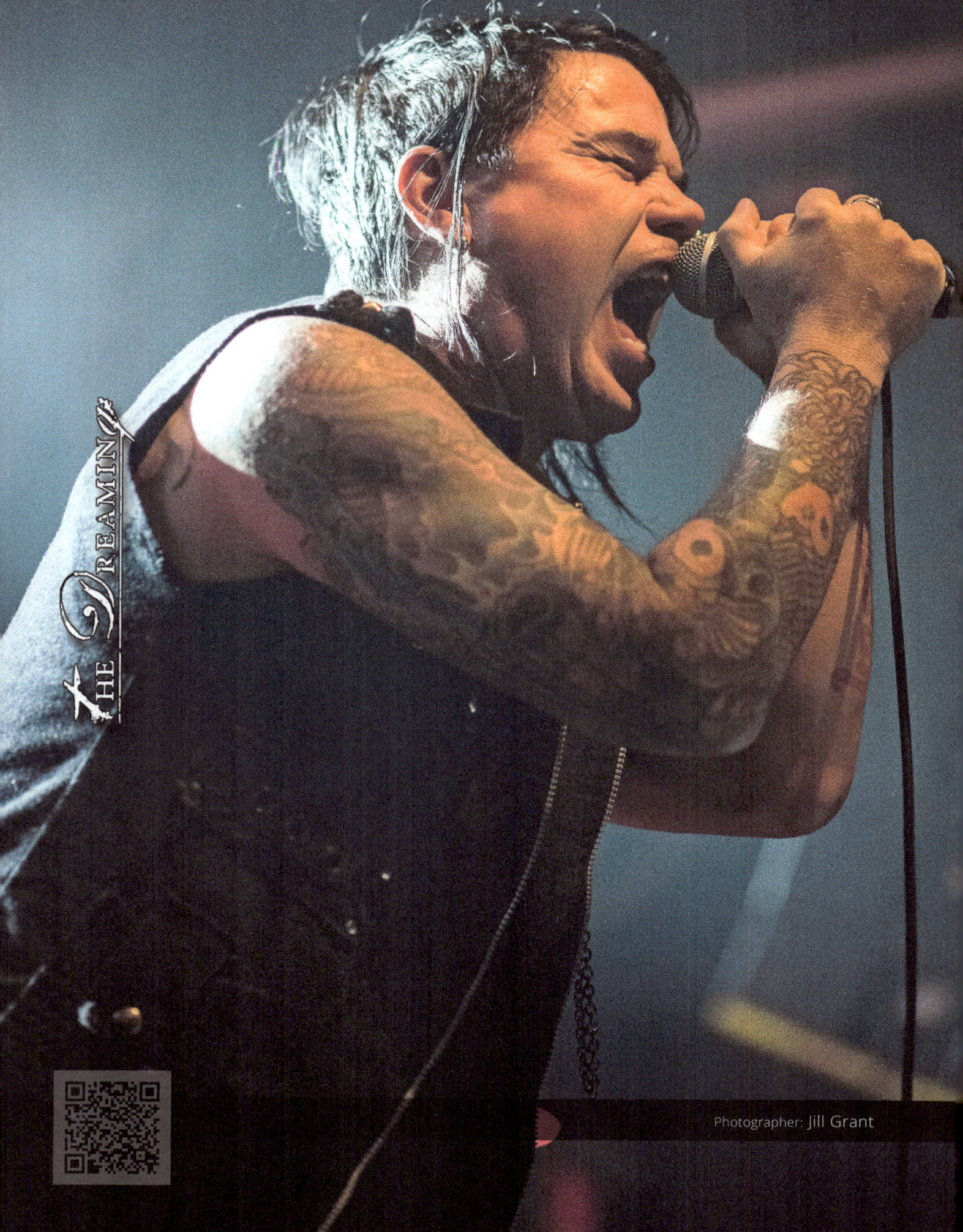

The Dreaming

Photographer: Jill Grant

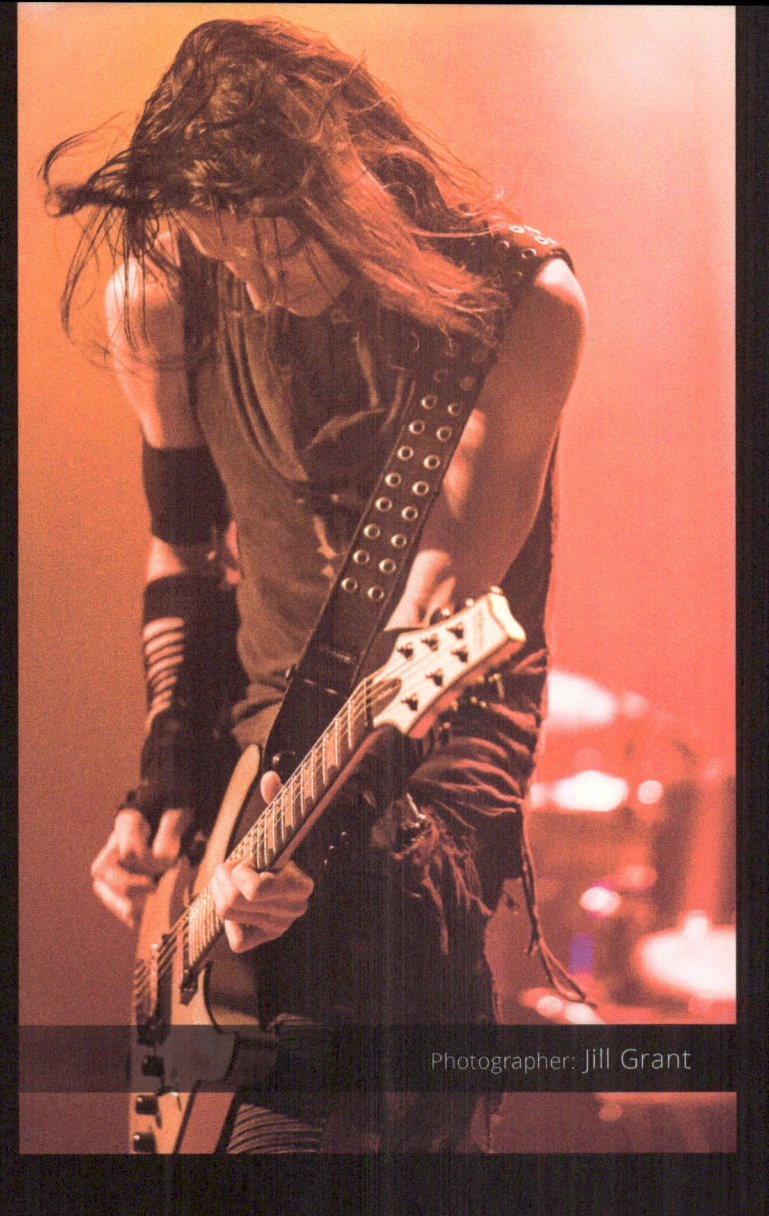

Photographer: Jill Grant

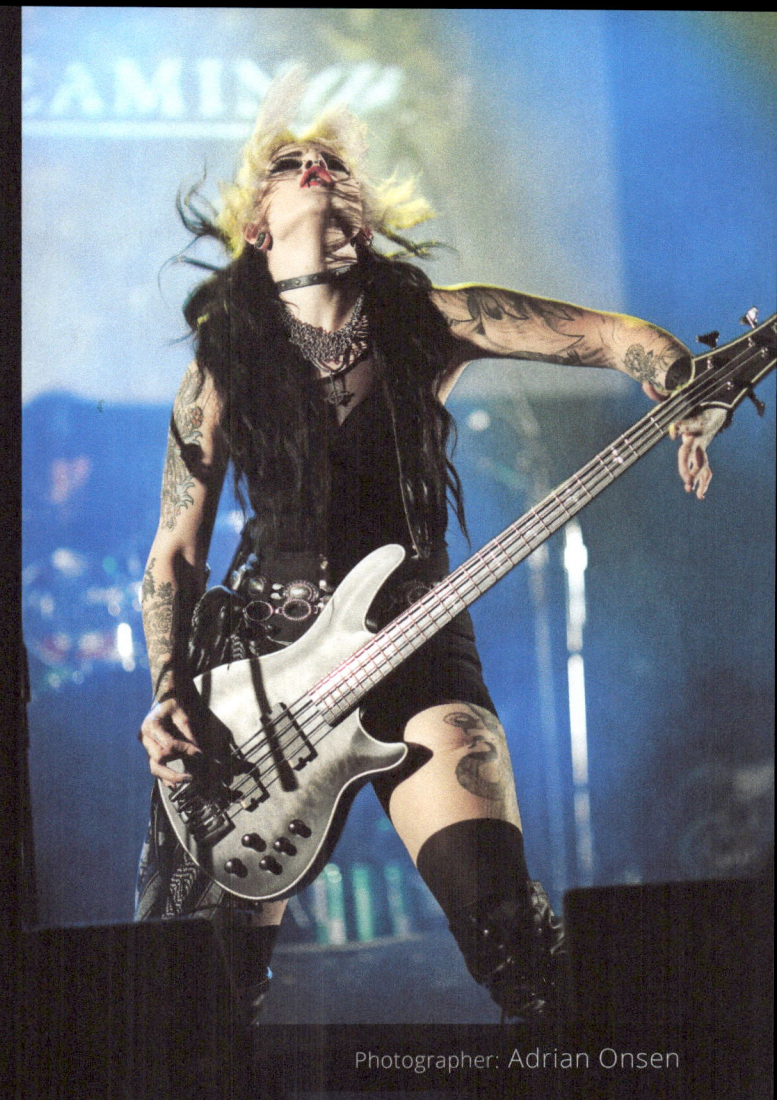

Photographer: Adrian Onsen

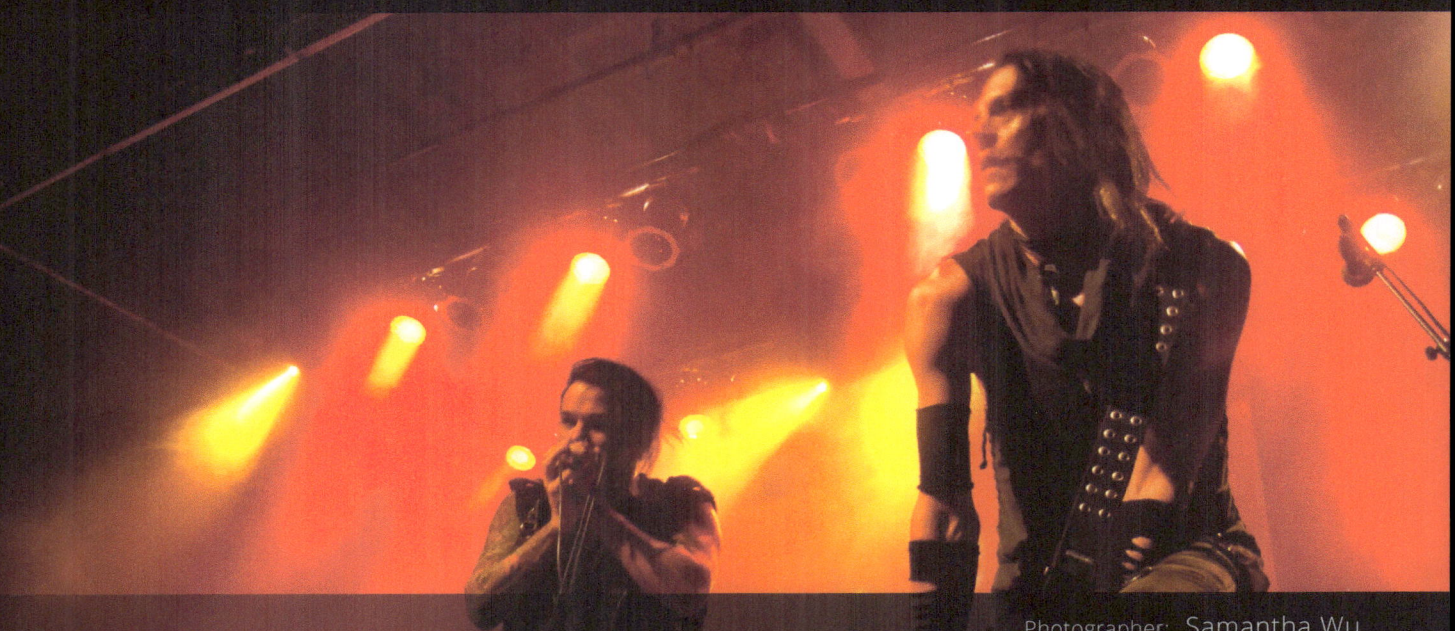

Photographer: Samantha Wu

19

BRUDERSCHAFT

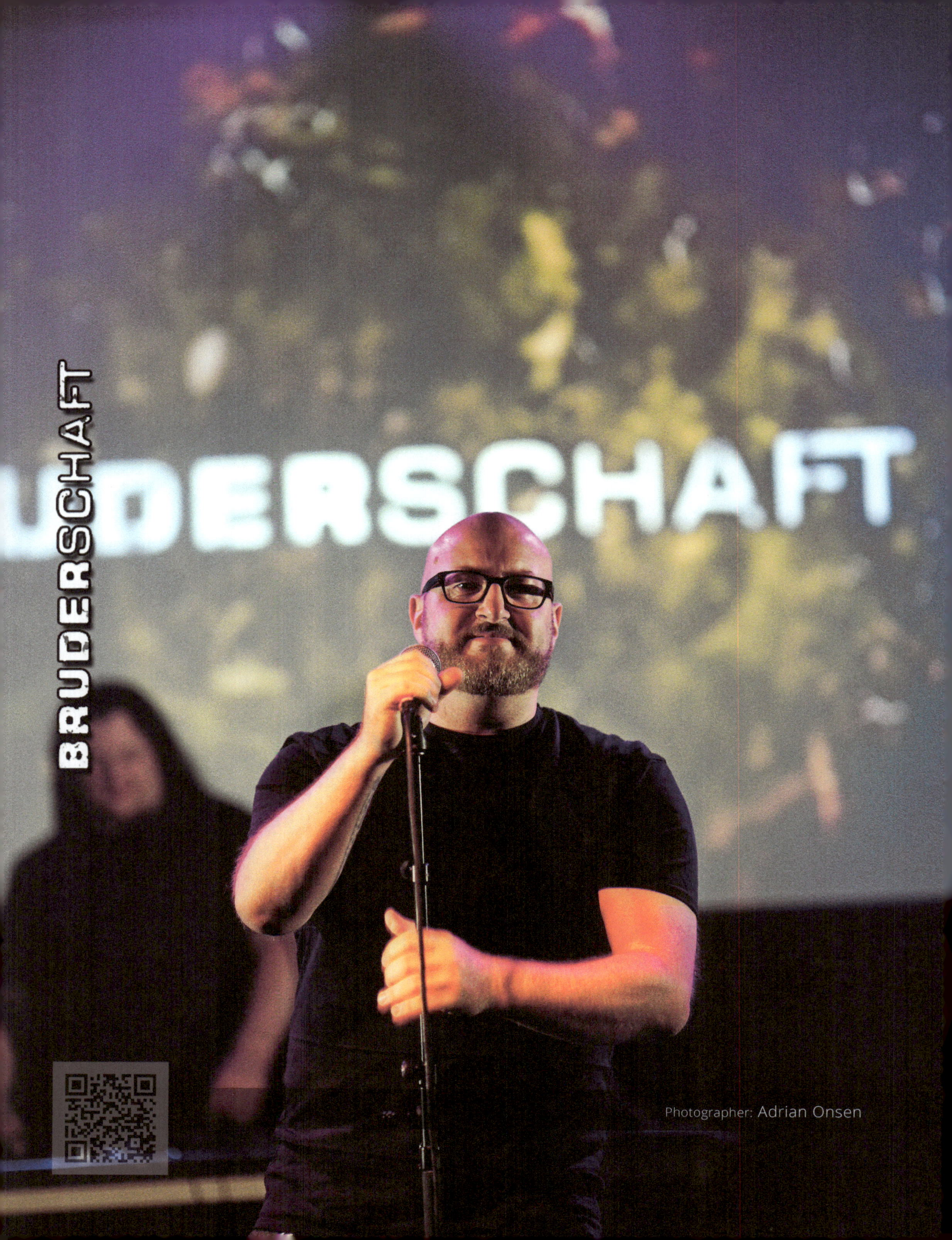

...UDERSCHAFT

Photographer: Adrian Onsen

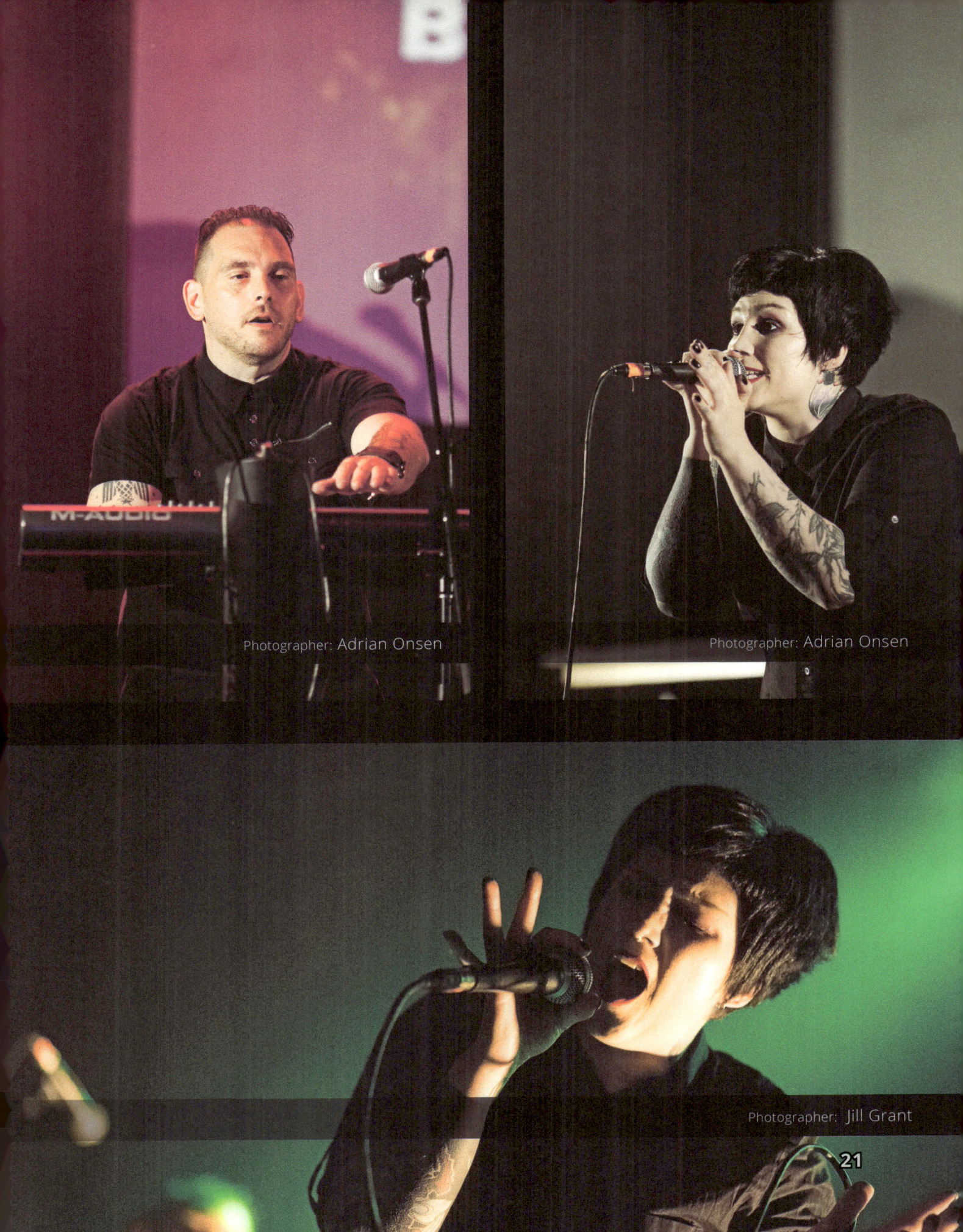

Photographer: Adrian Onsen

Photographer: Adrian Onsen

Photographer: Jill Grant

21

LE*A*ETHER STRIP

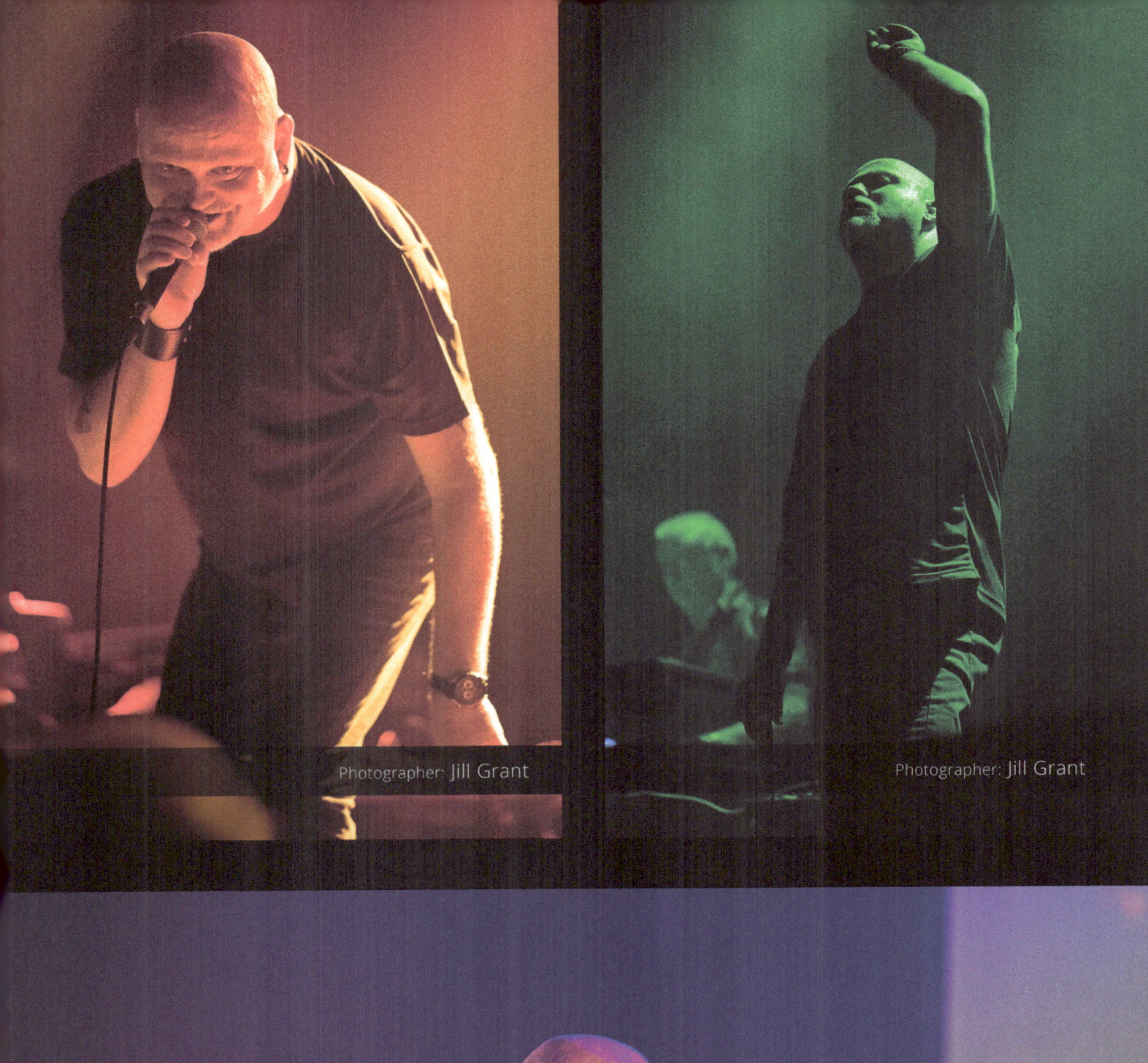

Photographer: Jill Grant

Photographer: Jill Grant

Photographer: Adrian Onsen

23

AFTERMATH

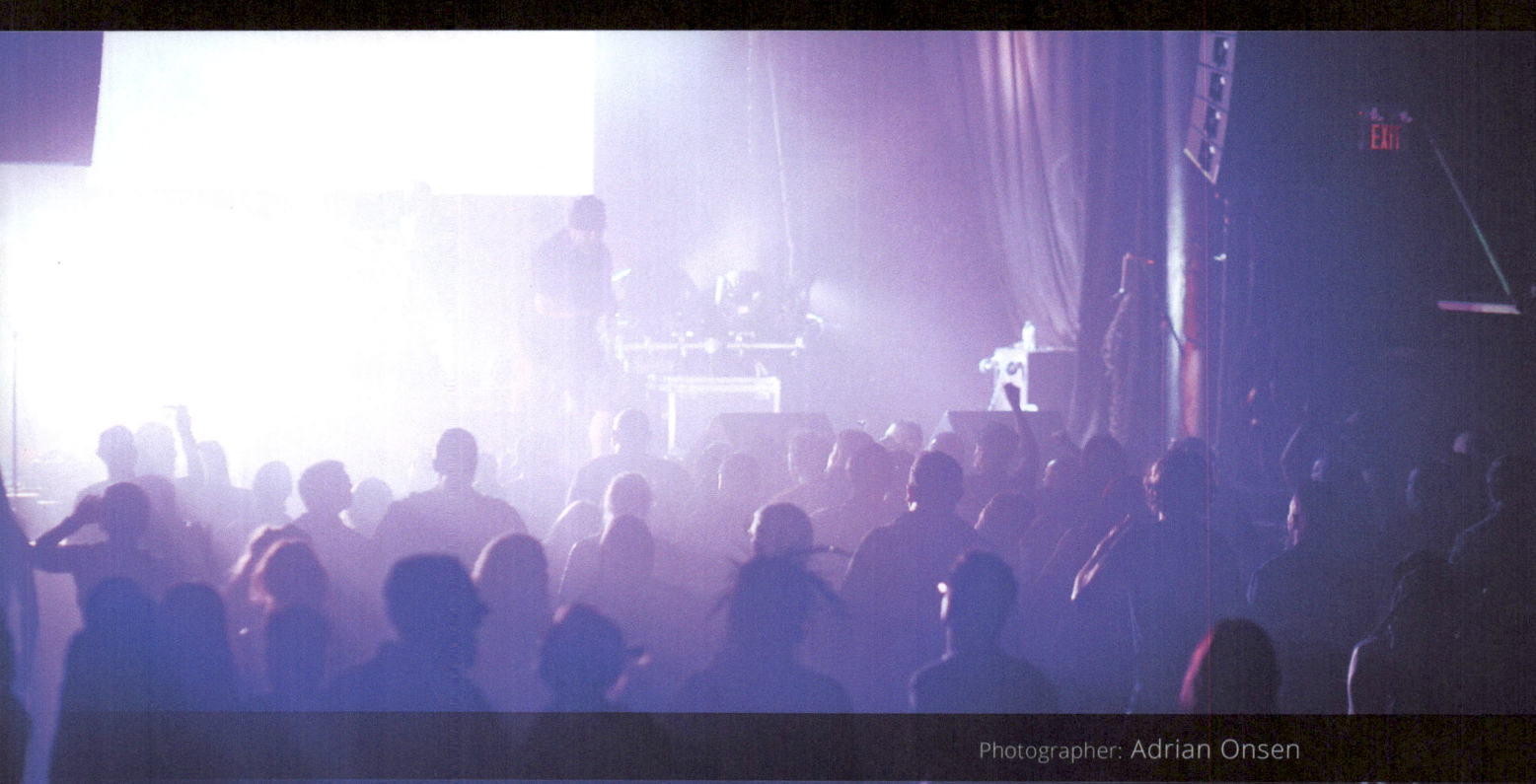

Photographer: Adrian Onsen

Day 2
Friday, 28 August, 2015

Dark electronic music is a nebulous concept. There are a few shared motifs and symbols that can be used to classify an act as such, but hardly any consensus exists on what to expect of the style. Aftermath performers have firmly rooted, idiosyncratic origins, yet they thrive through their defiance of established order.

In the grand context of musical arts, electronic instruments are a relative novelty. Yet in each subsequent decade since the theremin, distinct mainstreams have emerged, and from them, the dark side alternative genres. Dark electronic music thus refers not to what one might expect of the performances, but rather what not to expect: conformity and uniformity.

The rebels never stop rebelling. They strive for divergence and diversity.

The second day of Aftermath was a meticulously curated showcase of classic and experimental extremes. It was a thrilling juxtaposition of tributes and innovative visions. The artists paid homage to their origins and the electronic revolutionaries who inspired them, then launched into uncharted.and chaotic soundscapes.

Dead on TV
Stoneburner
Kevorkian Death Cycle
Nitro/Noise
Mr.Kitty
Ludovico Technique
Tactical Sekt
Velvet Acid Christ

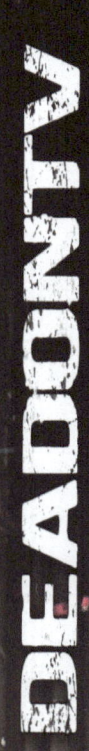

DEADONTV

Photographer: Adrian Onsen

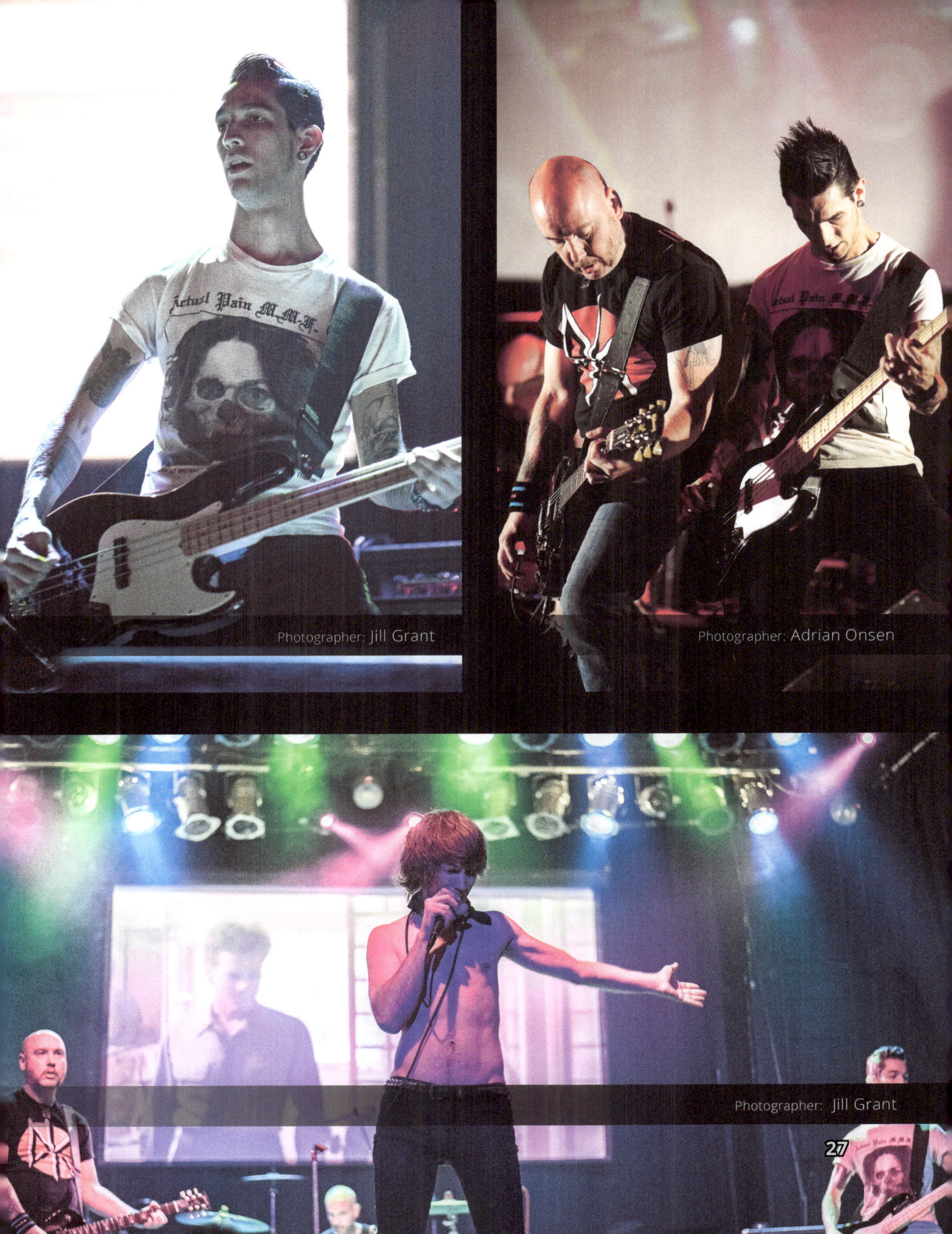

Photographer: Jill Grant

Photographer: Adrian Onsen

Photographer: Jill Grant

27

STONEBURNER

Photographer: Adrian Onsen

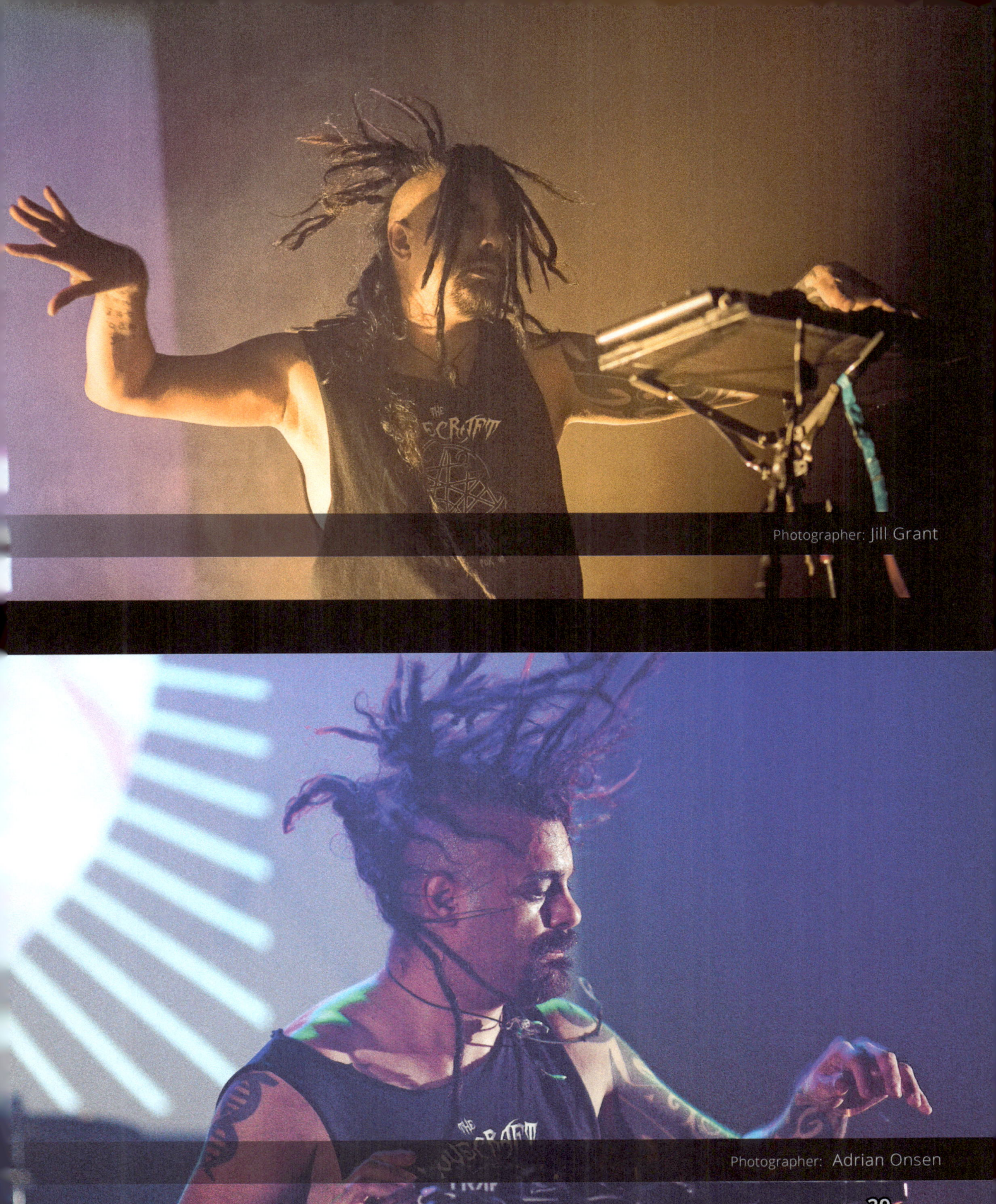

Photographer: Jill Grant

Photographer: Adrian Onsen

29

KEVORKIAN
DEATHCYCLE

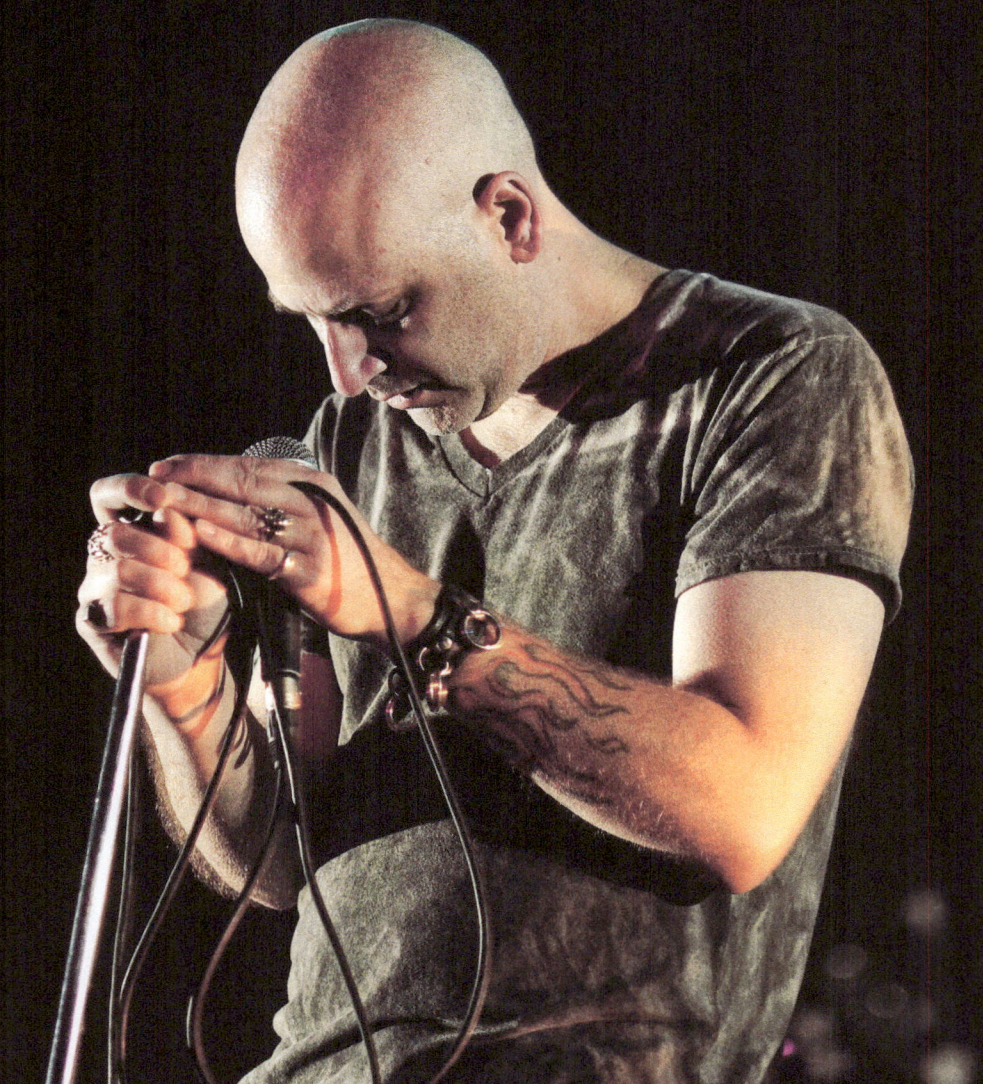

Photographer: Adrian Onsen

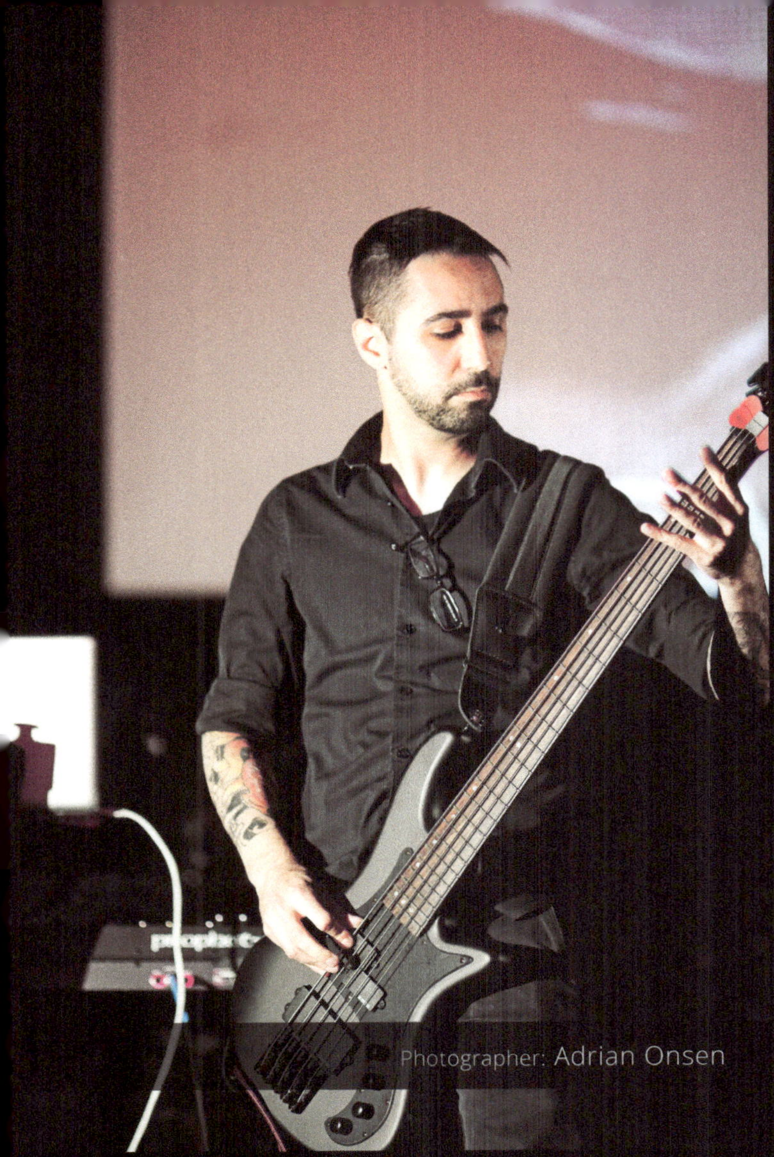

Photographer: Adrian Onsen

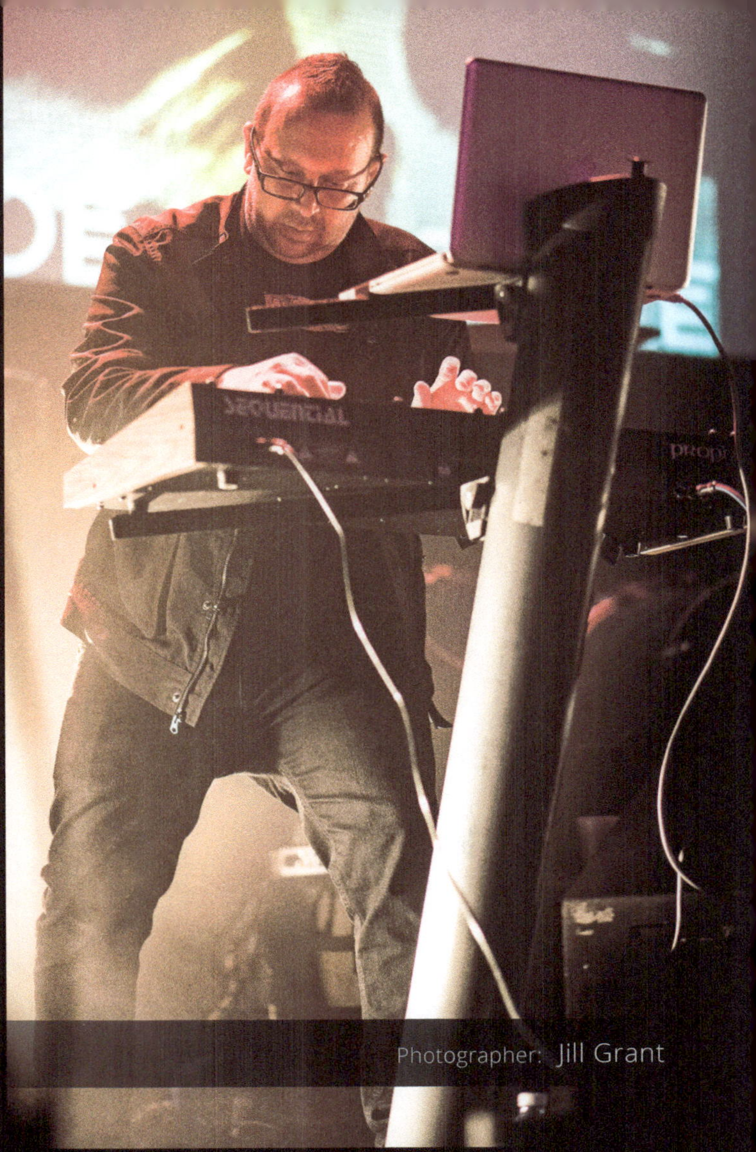

Photographer: Jill Grant

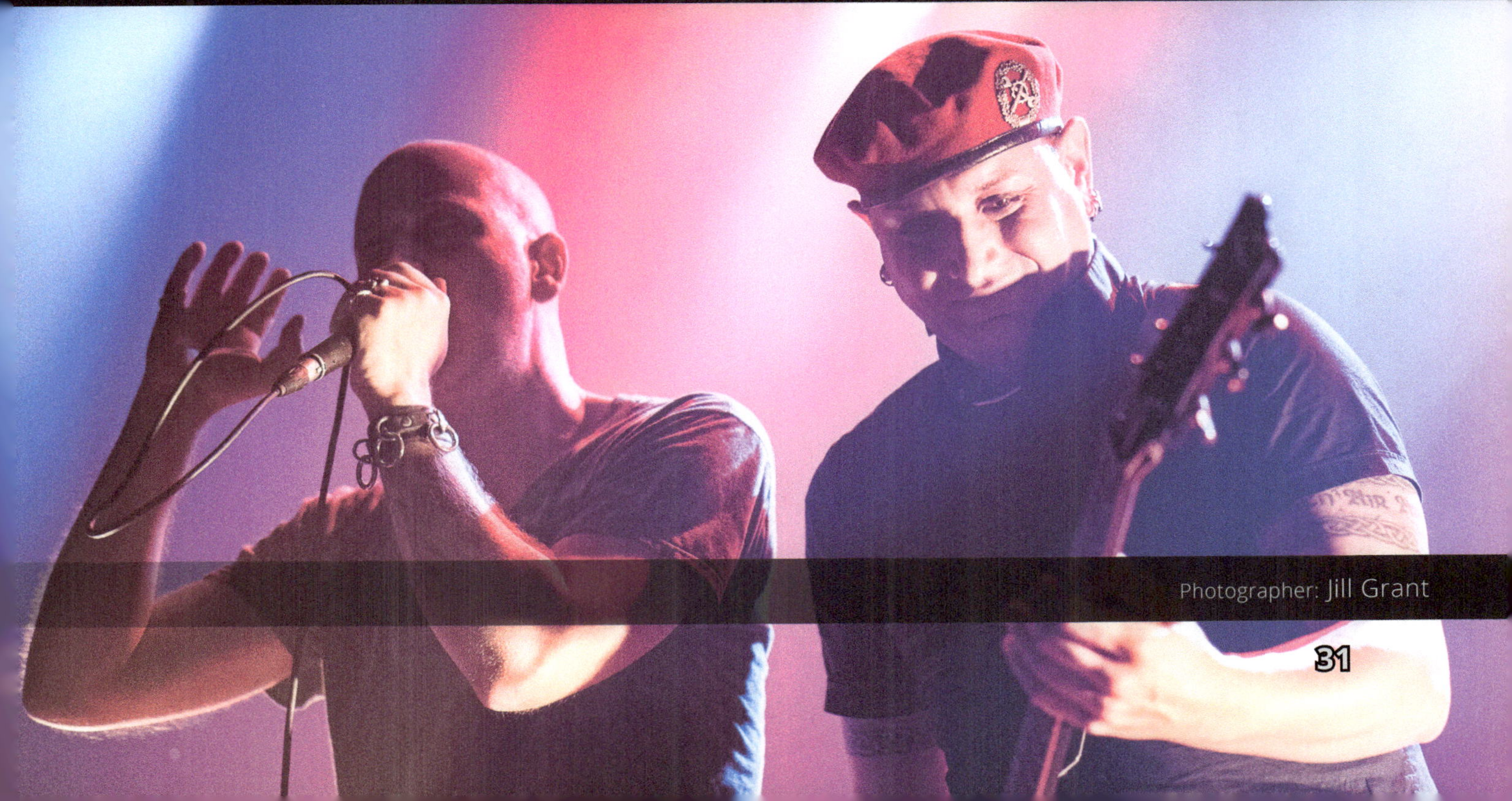

Photographer: Jill Grant

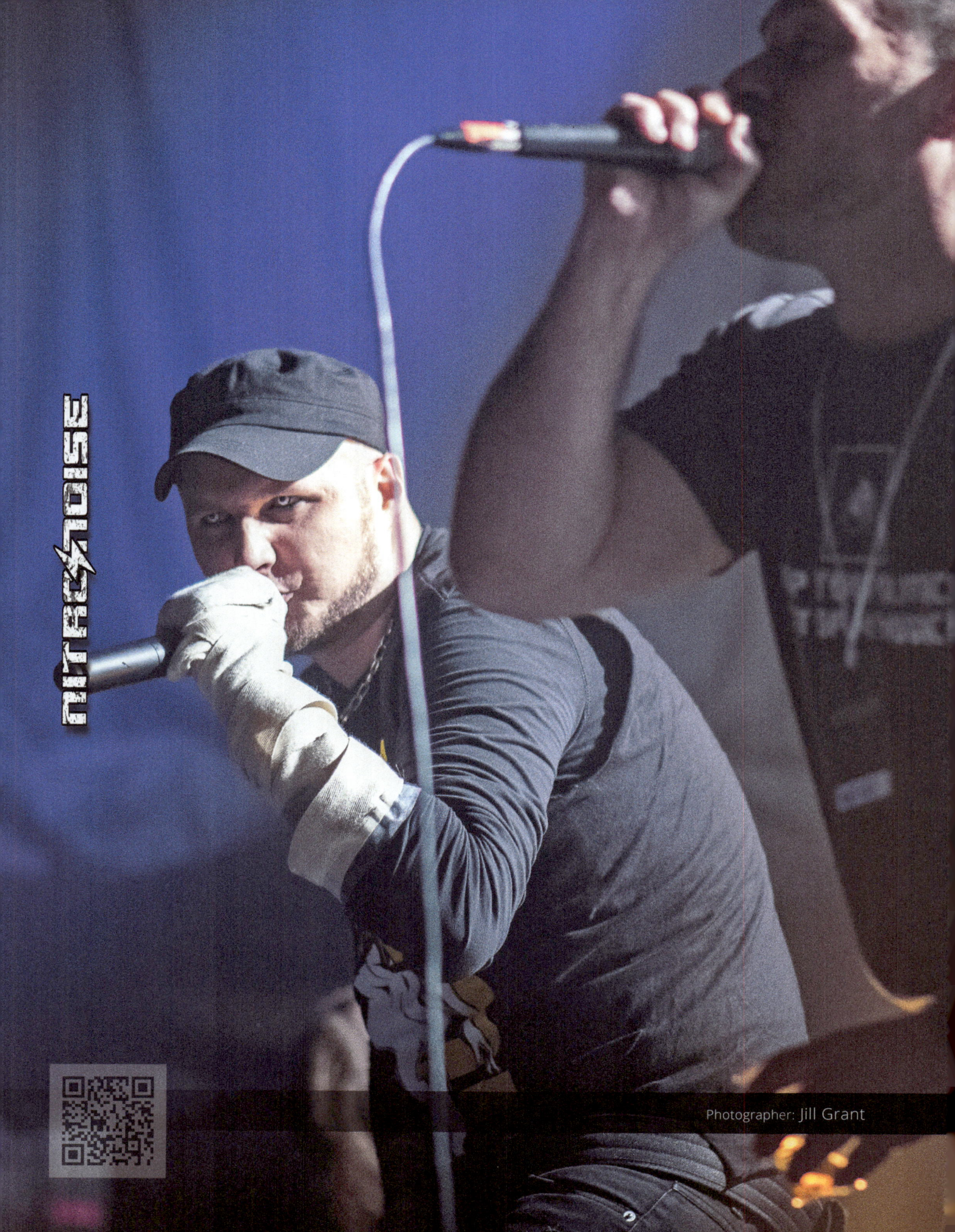

NITRONOISE

Photographer: Jill Grant

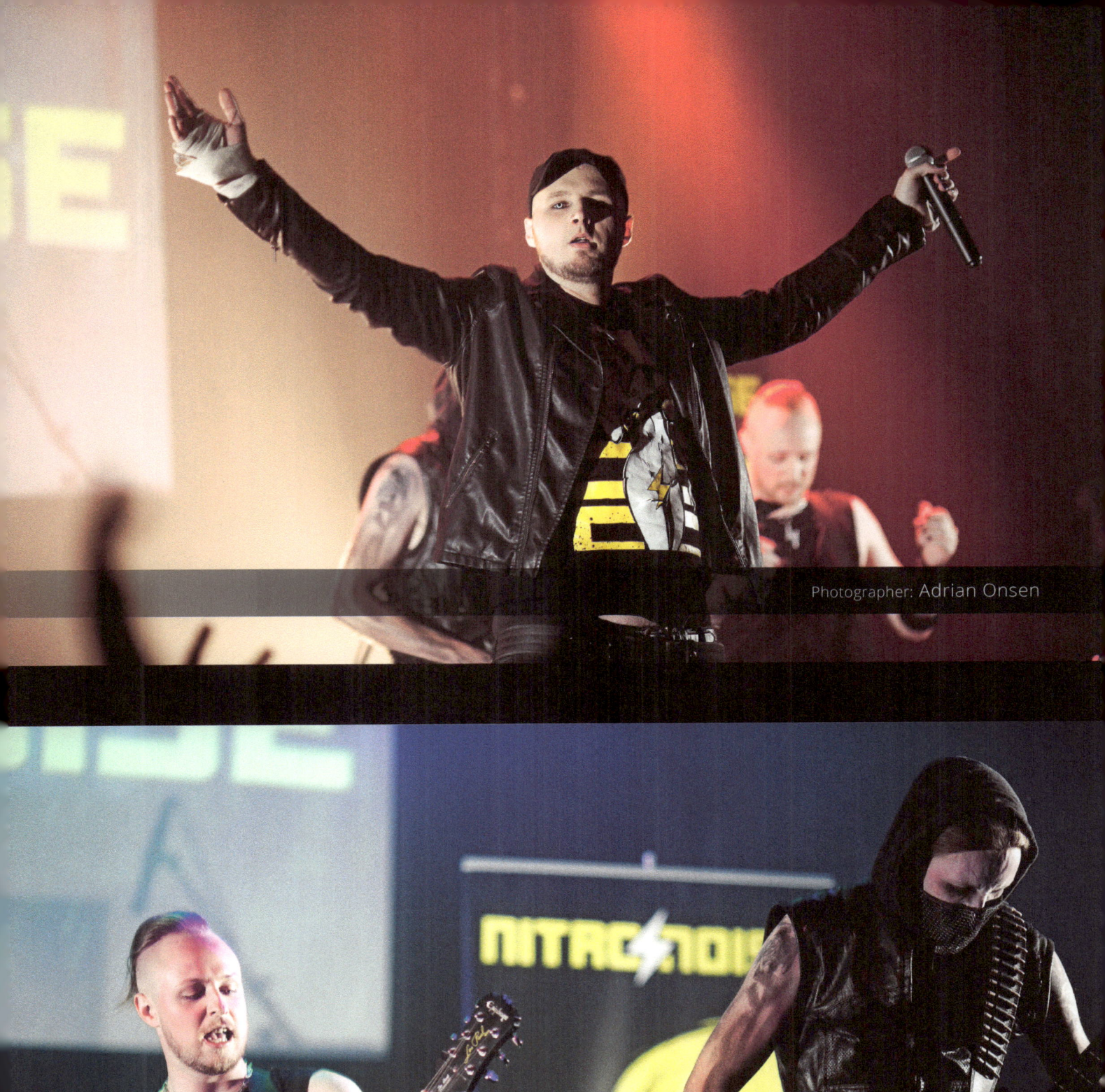

Photographer: Adrian Onsen

Photographer: Adrian Onsen

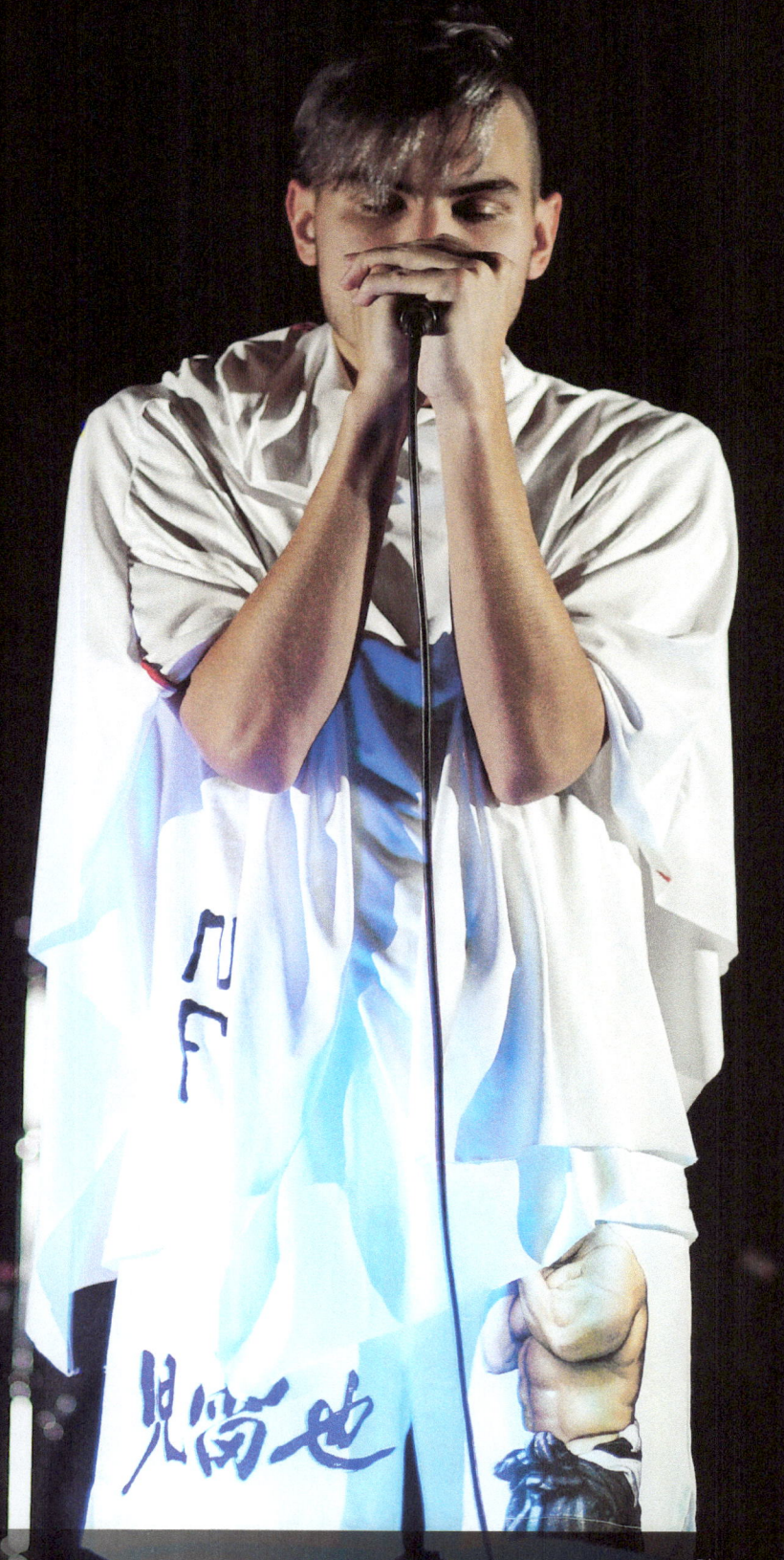

MR. KITTY

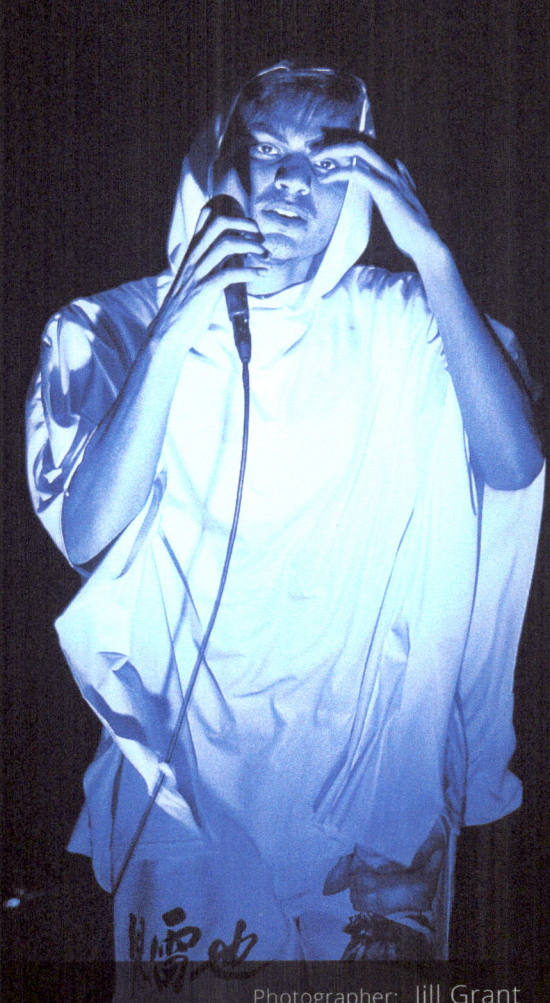

Photographer: Jill Grant

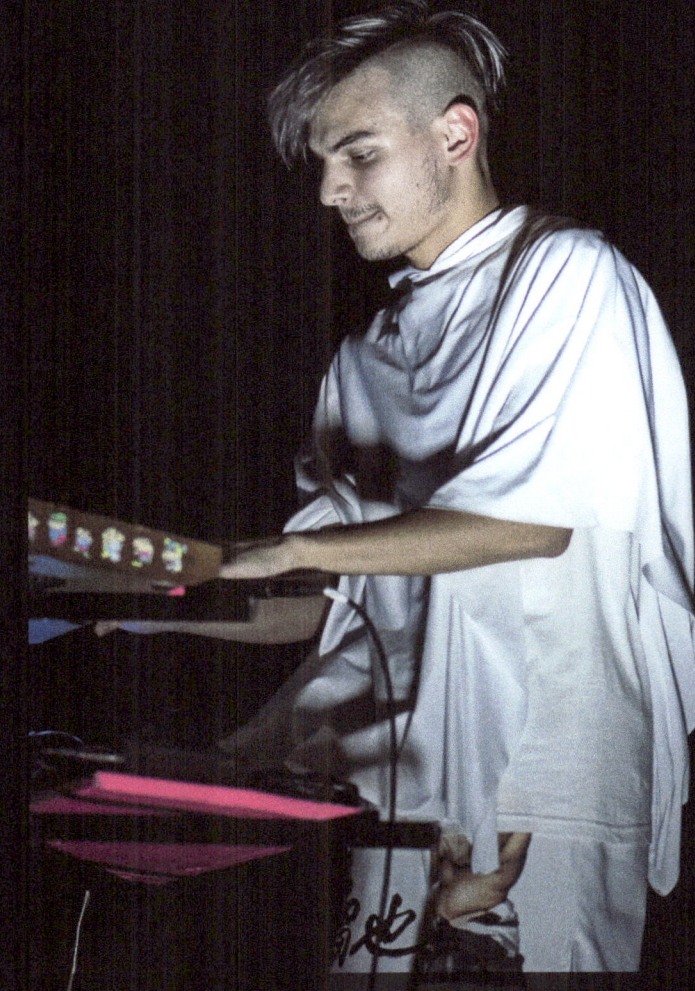

Photographer: Jill Grant

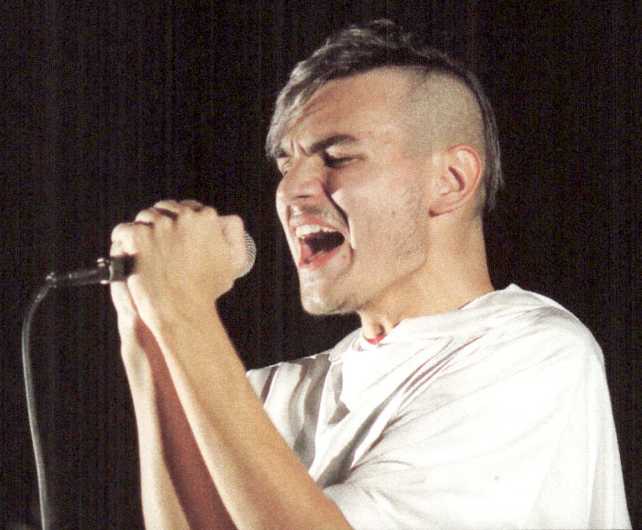

Photographer: Adrian Onsen

35

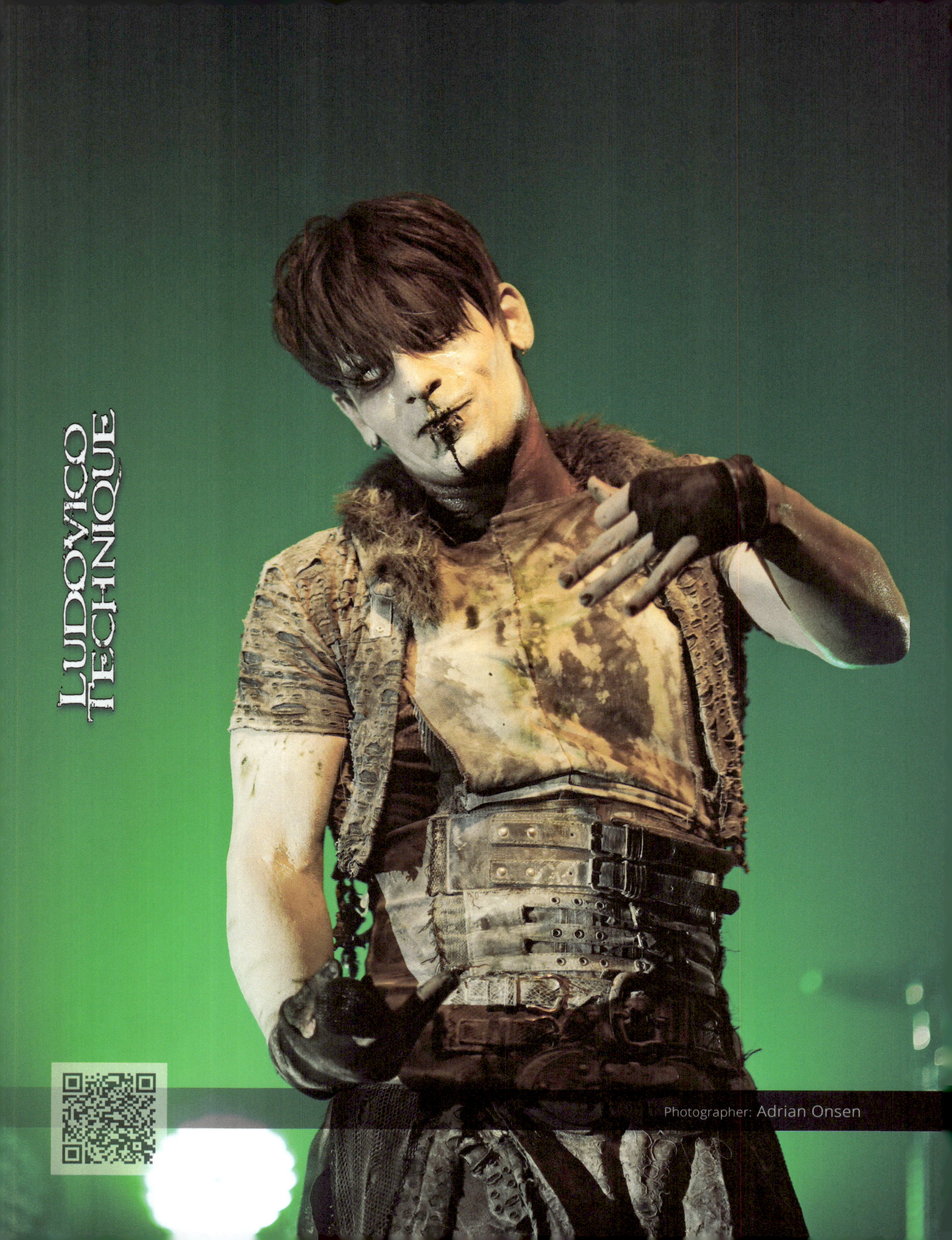

LUDOVICO TECHNIQUE

Photographer: Adrian Onsen

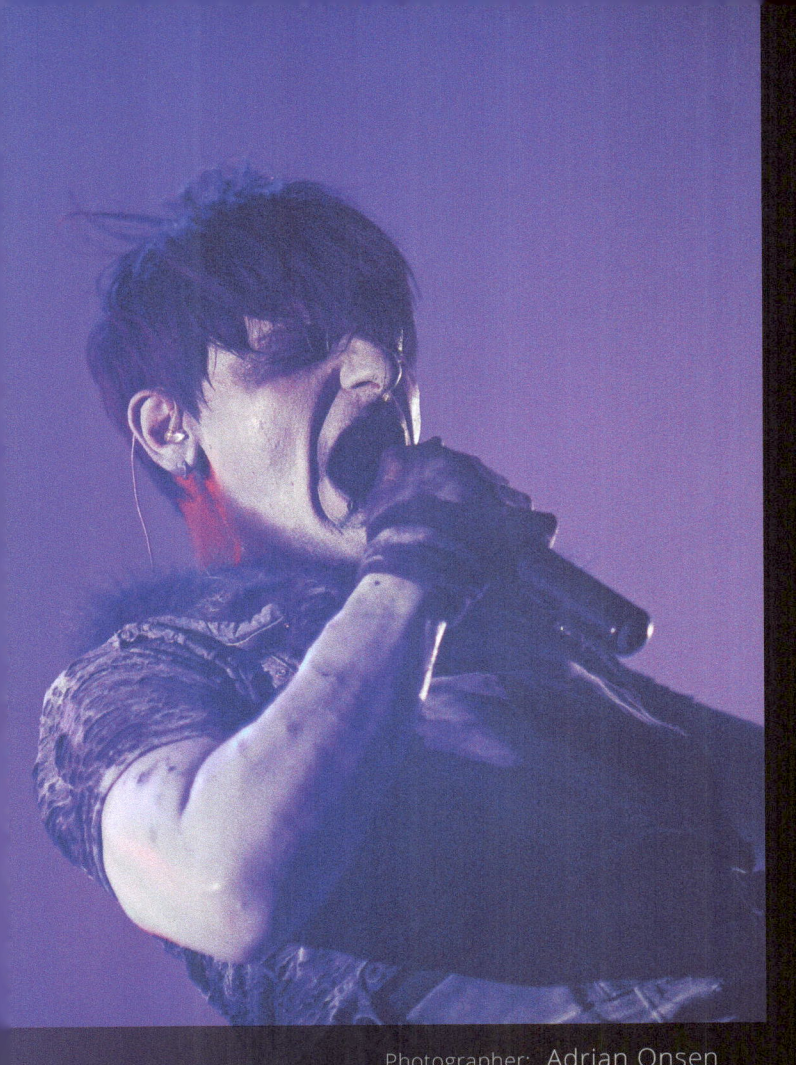

Photographer: Adrian Onsen

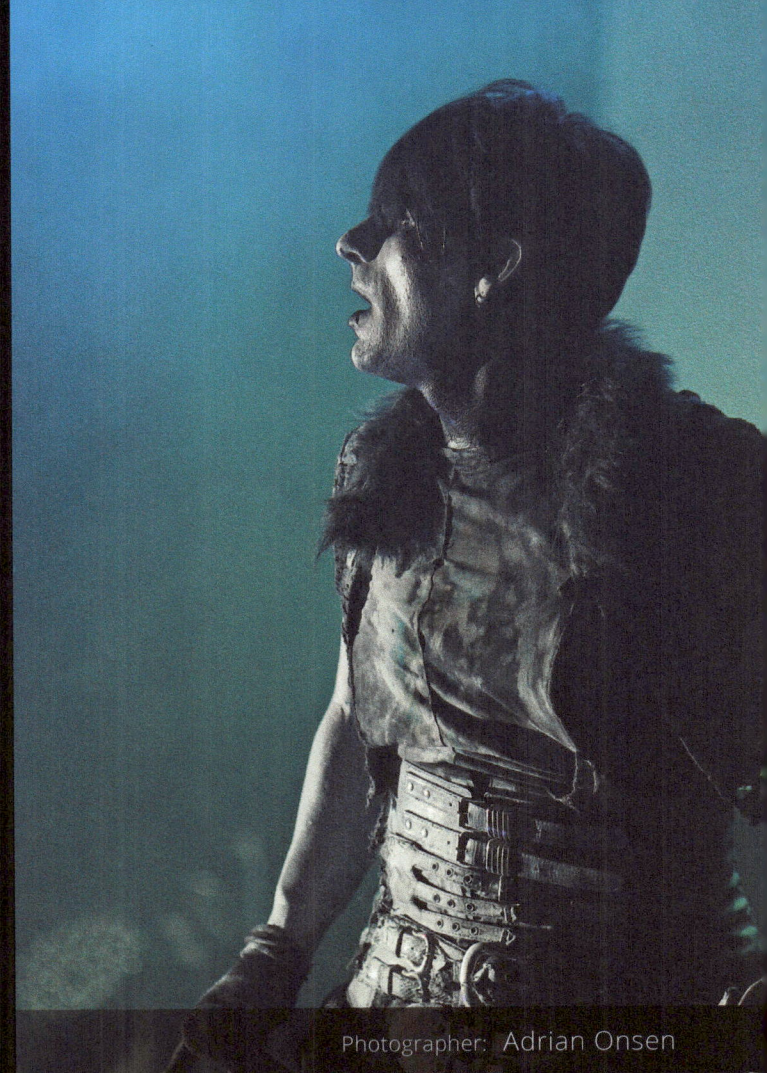

Photographer: Adrian Onsen

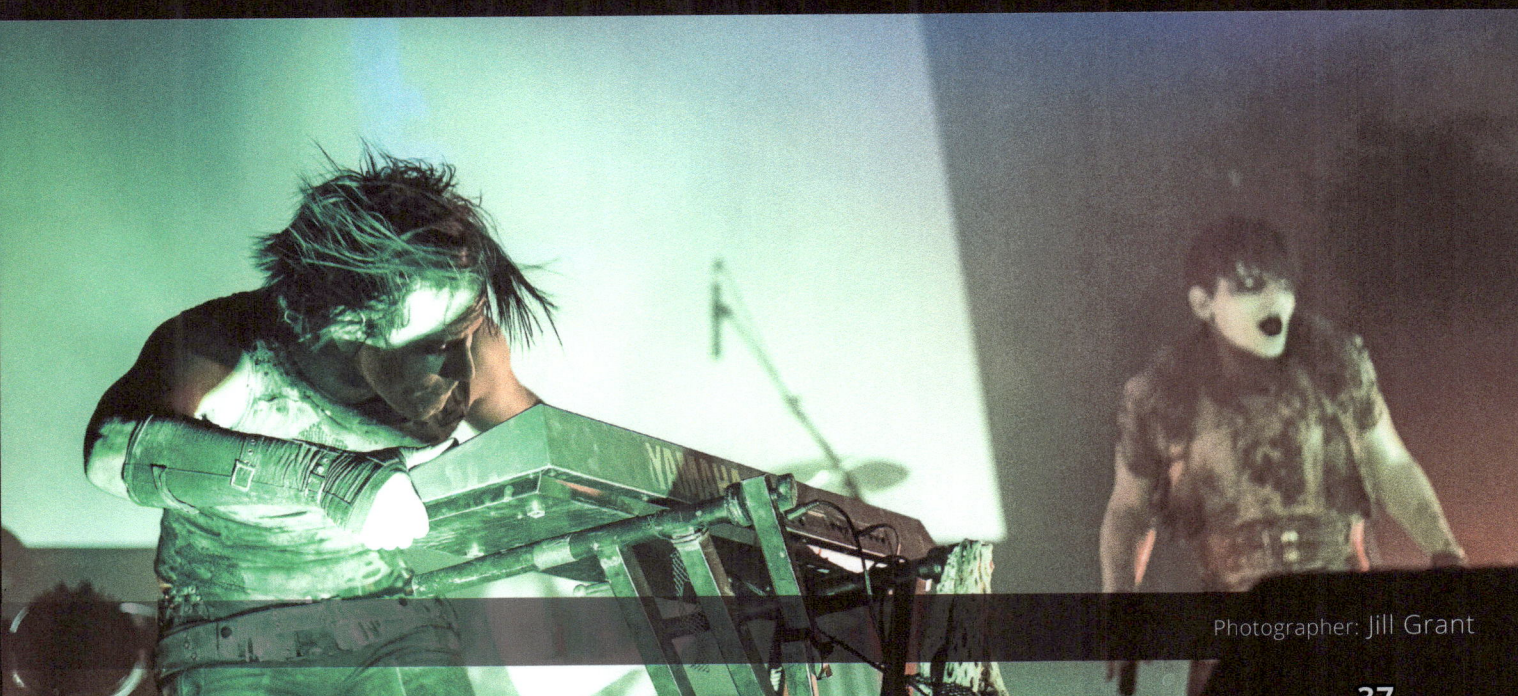

Photographer: Jill Grant

37

TACTICAL SEKT

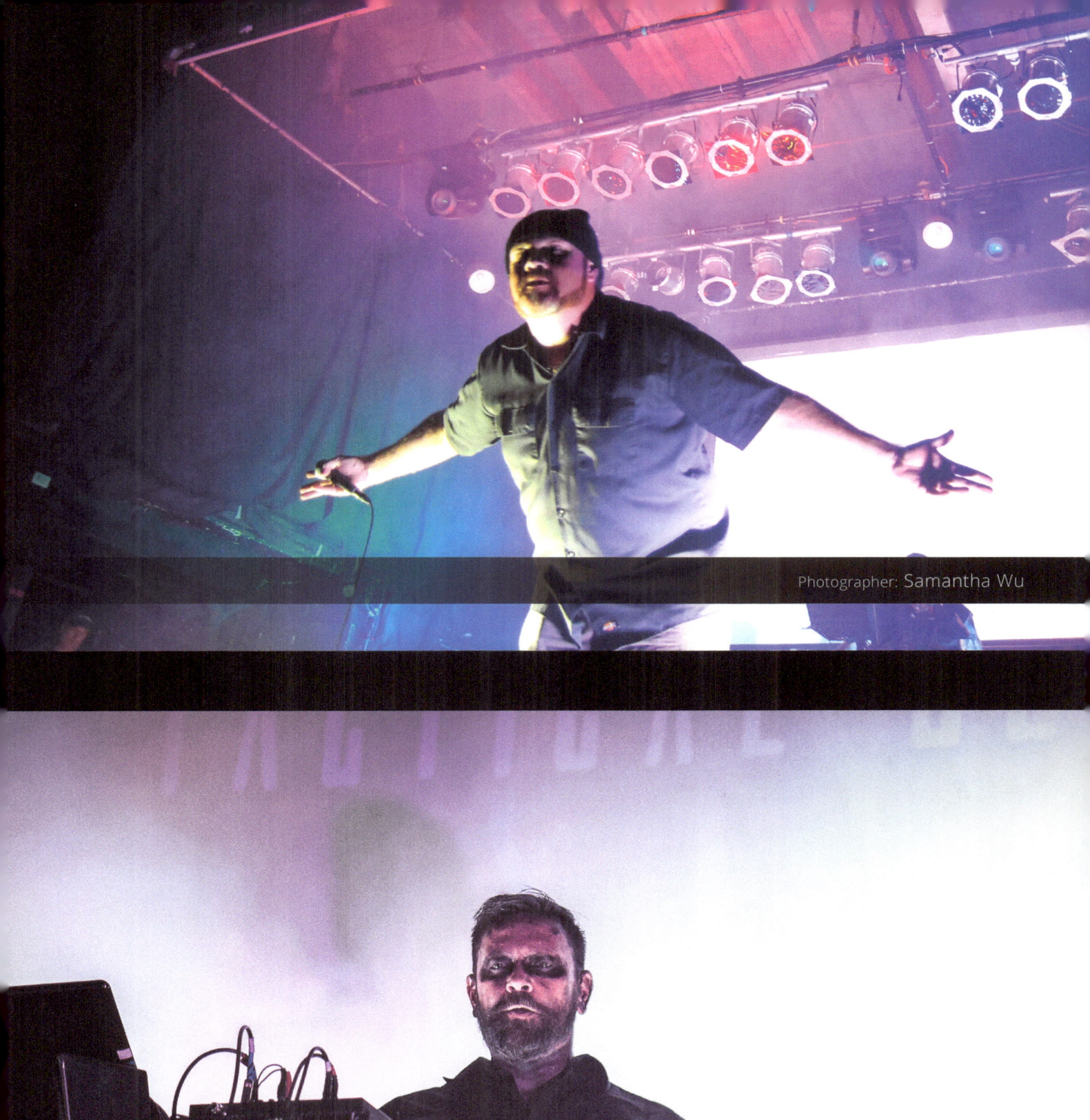

Photographer: Samantha Wu

Photographer: Jill Grant

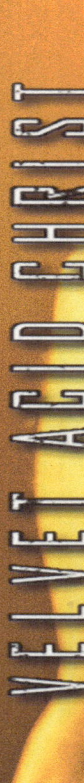

VELVET ACID CHRIST

Photographer: Jill Grant

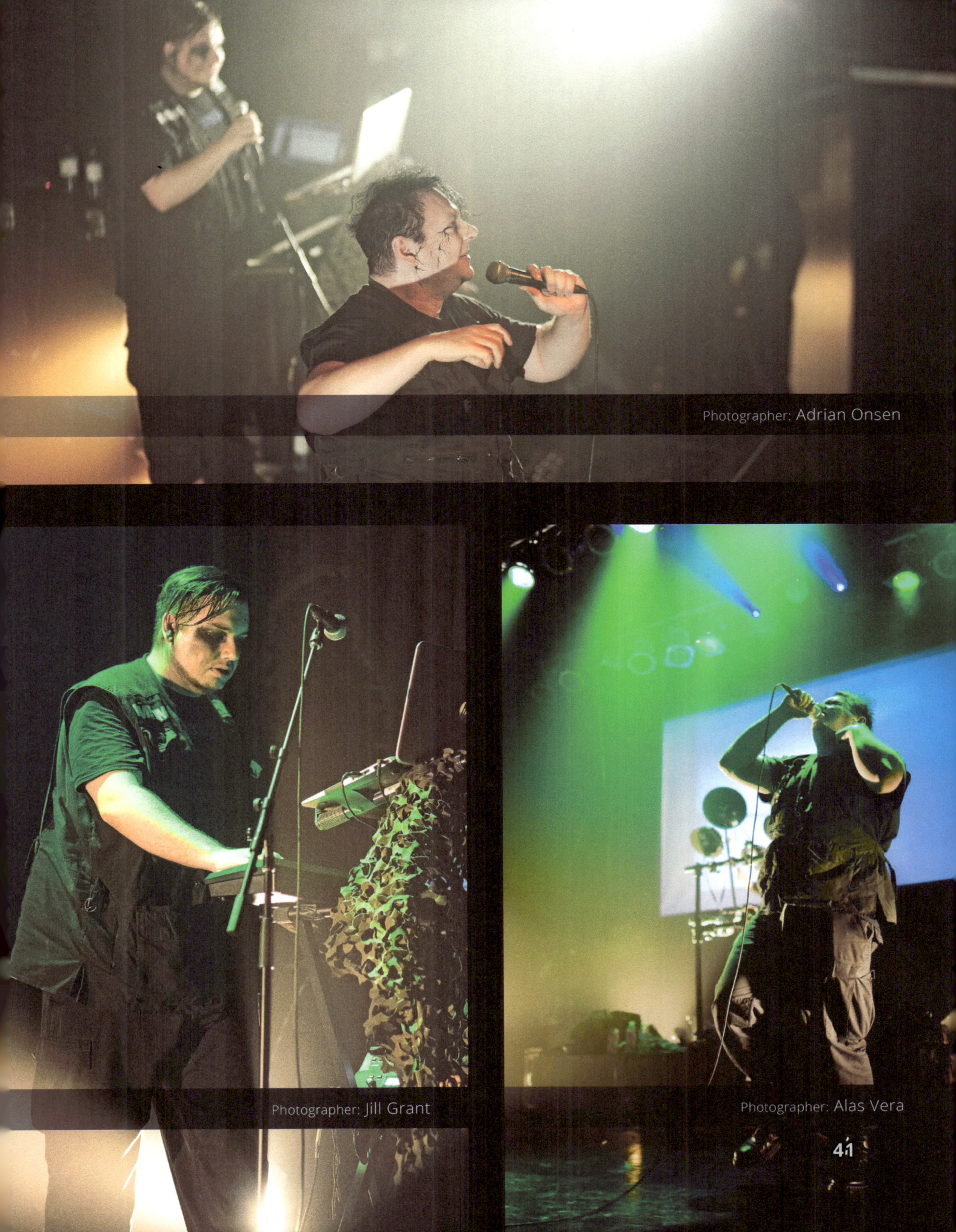

Photographer: Adrian Onsen

Photographer: Jill Grant

Photographer: Alas Vera

41

AFTERMATH

Photographer: Adrian Onsen

Day 3
Saturday, 29 August, 2015

Many of the Aftermath artists reject labels, producing revolutionary aesthetics and sounds. Musical styles evolve by intercepting contemporary influences to create potent new wells of inspiration.

This is characteristic to all postmodern art: perpetually divergent genres, the fragmentation of traditional form and function due to our access to global communication networks. Artists in disparate domains are closer than ever before in history. They have the unprecedented freedom to collaborate and conspire, to enrich each other's style.

Openness to genre alliance and synthesis make festivals like Aftermath an exquisite palimpsest of decades in alternative electronic music; the sounds were familiar, yet simultaneously abstract and experimental.

Saturday night was a polychromatic extravagance, an unprecedented spectacle of cutting-edge performances. Limelight turned to black light and the Phoenix stage transformed into an enchanted forest and a battleground by turns. Strange, otherworldly apparitions tantalized the audience and brought them into the festival's frenzied climax.

Glenn Love
Electrovot
Mend
Squid Lid
GoFight
3TEETH
Conjure One
Haujobb

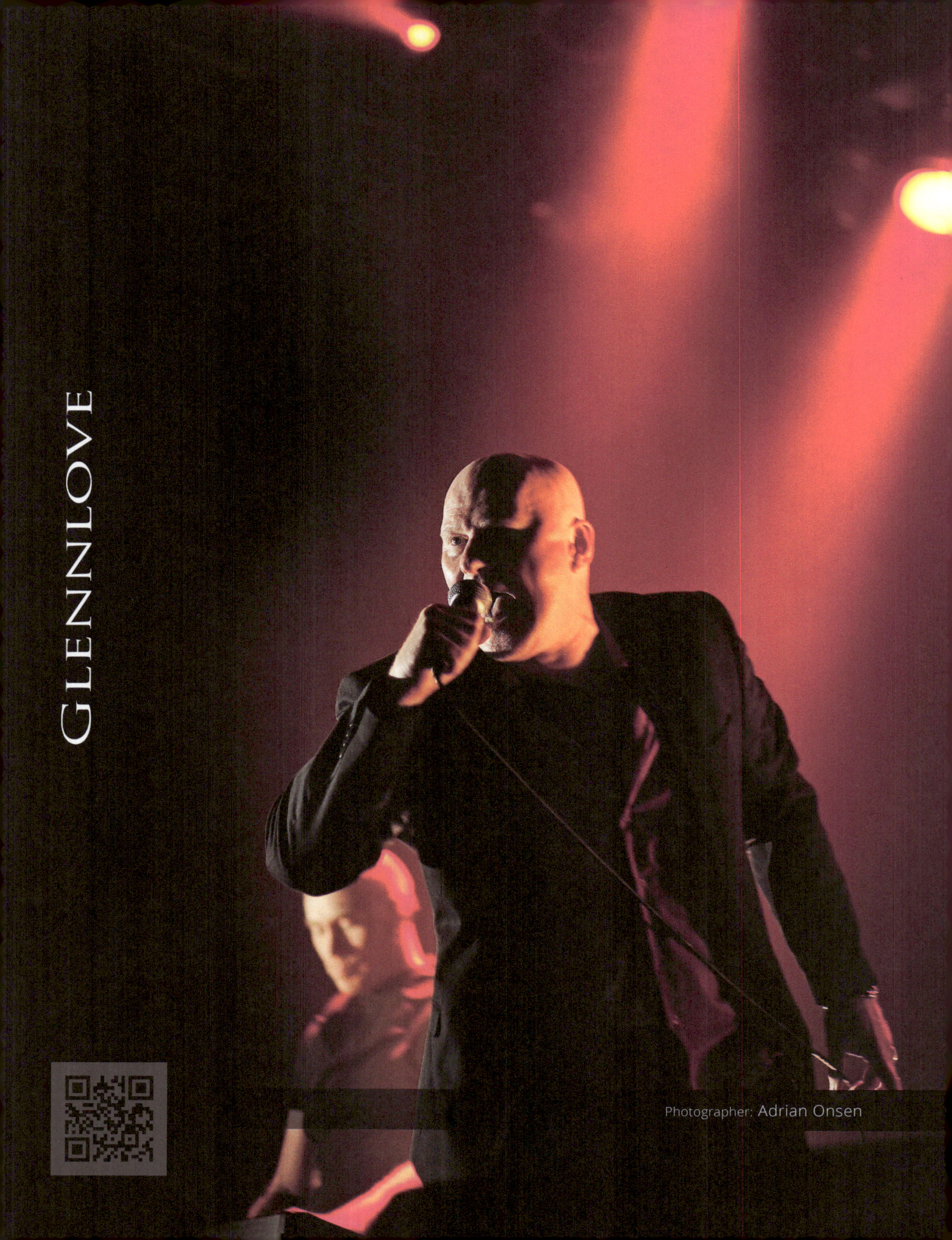

GLENNLOVE

Photographer: Adrian Onsen

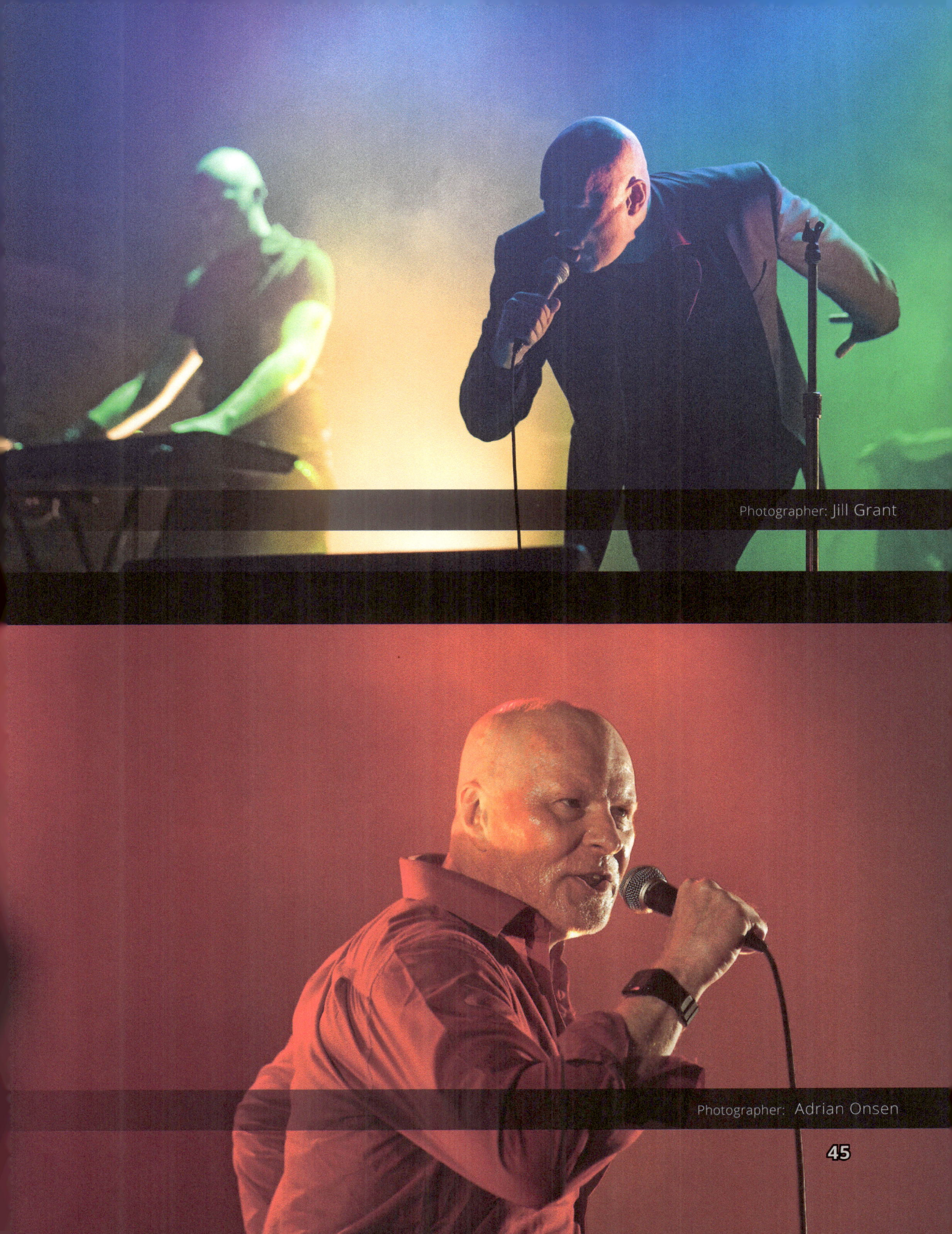

Photographer: Jill Grant

Photographer: Adrian Onsen

45

ELECTROVOT

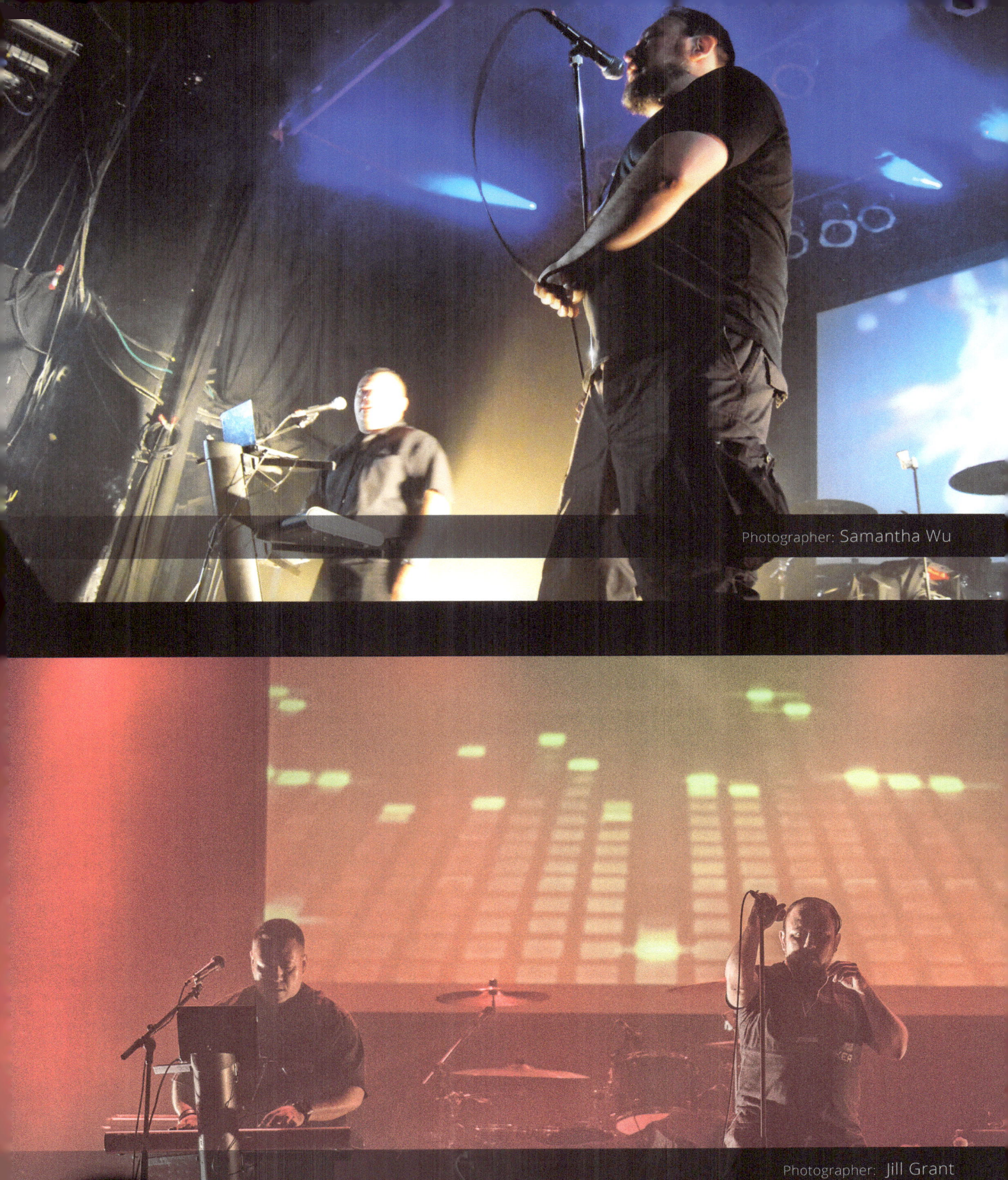

Photographer: Samantha Wu

Photographer: Jill Grant

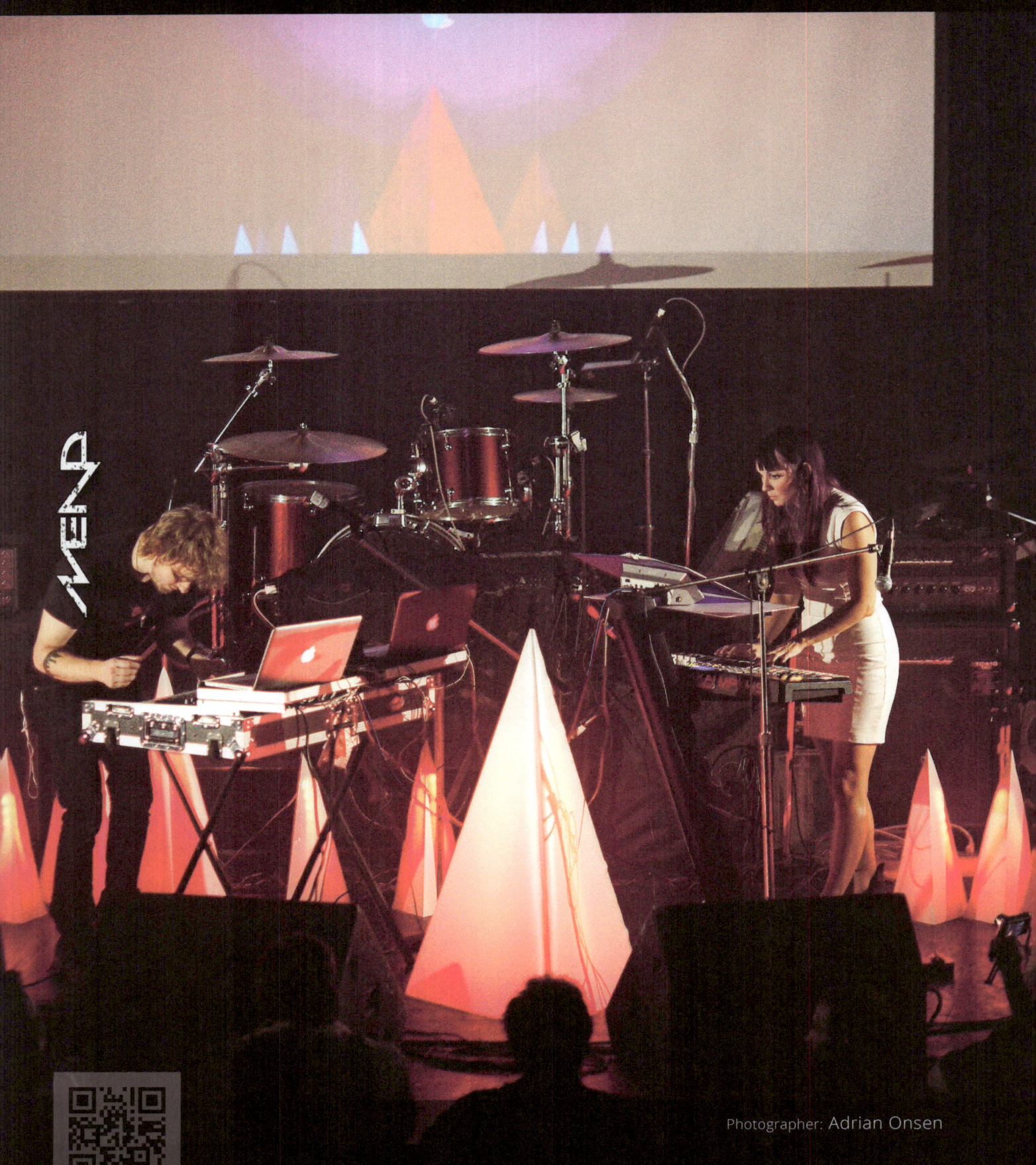

Photographer: Adrian Onsen

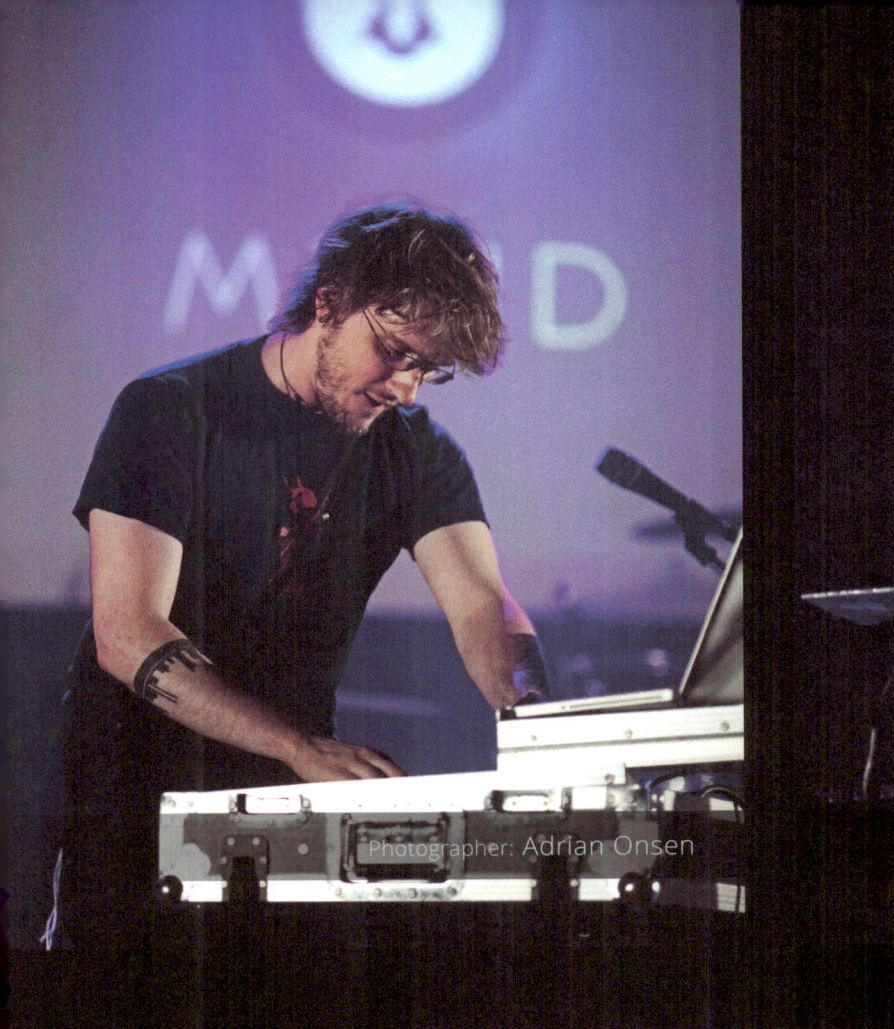

Photographer: Adrian Onsen

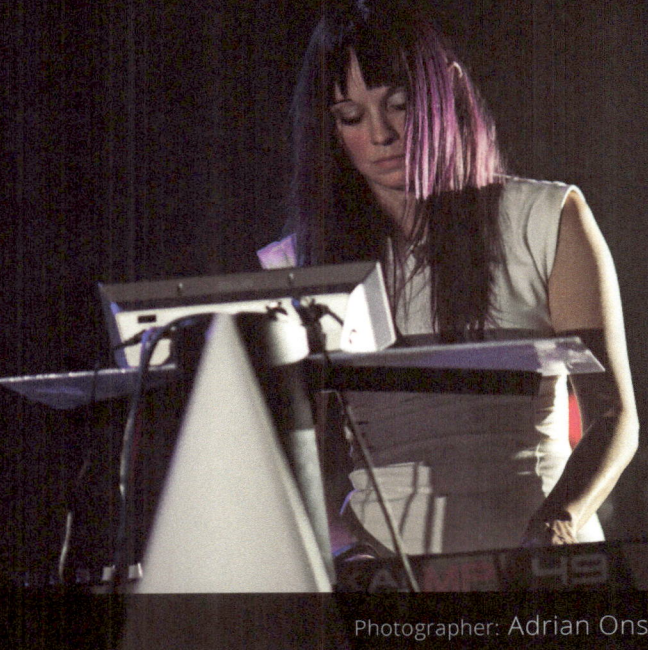

Photographer: Adrian Onsen

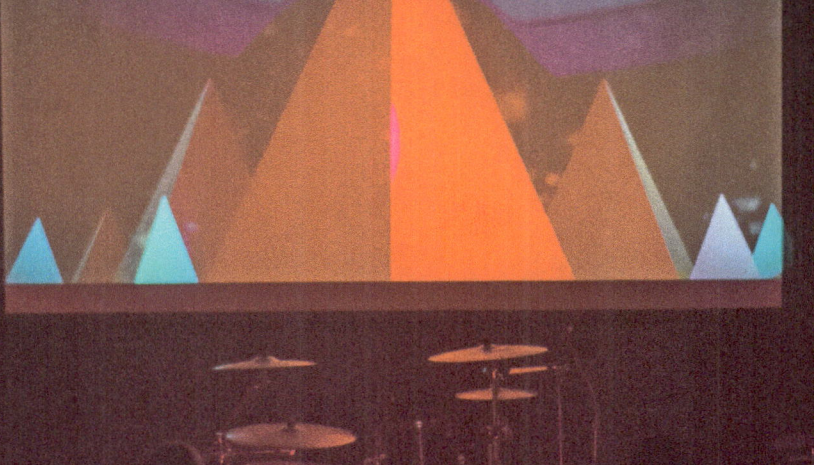

Photographer: Jill Grant

SQUID LID

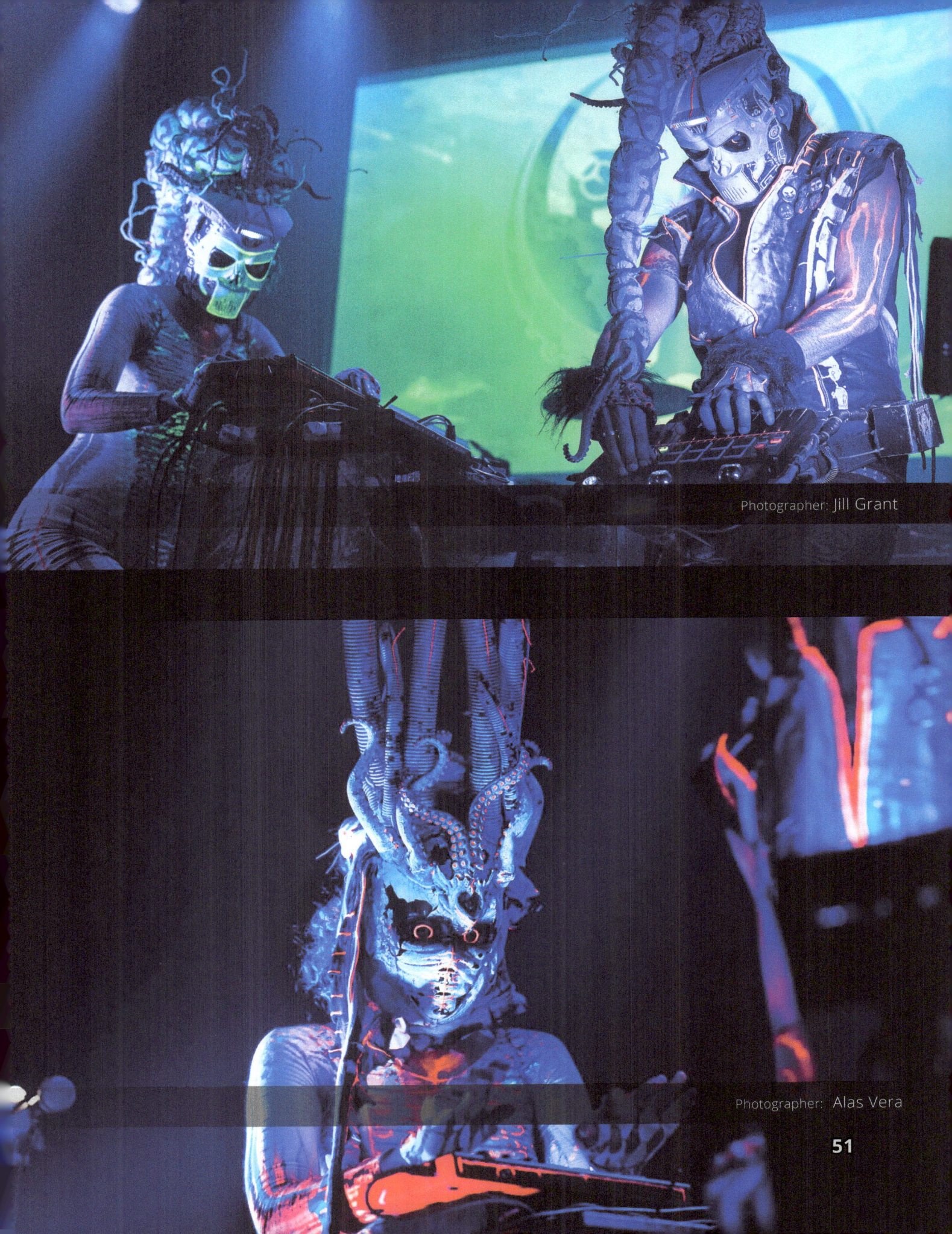

Photographer: Jill Grant

Photographer: Alas Vera

51

gofight

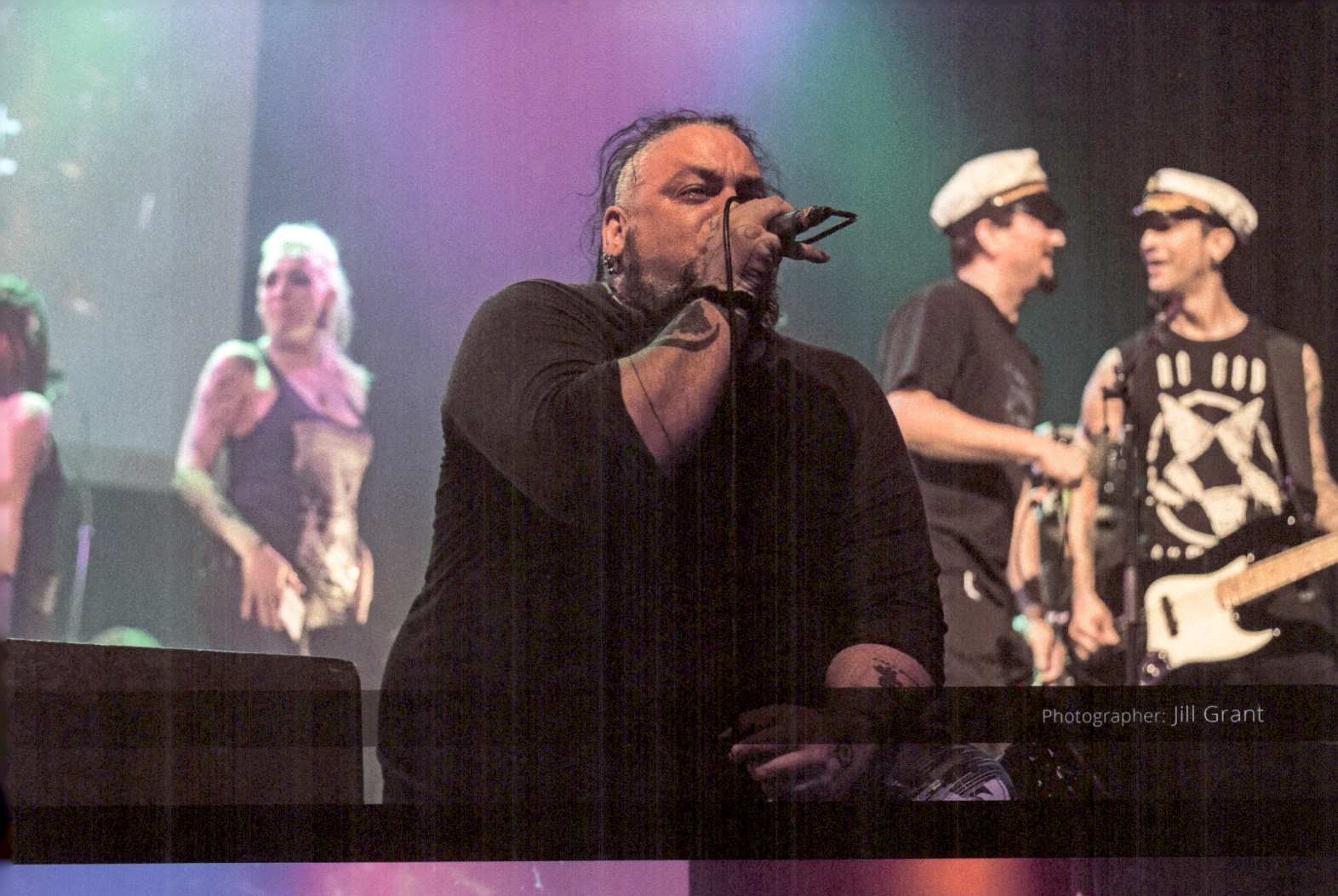

Photographer: Jill Grant

fight

Photographer: Alas Vera

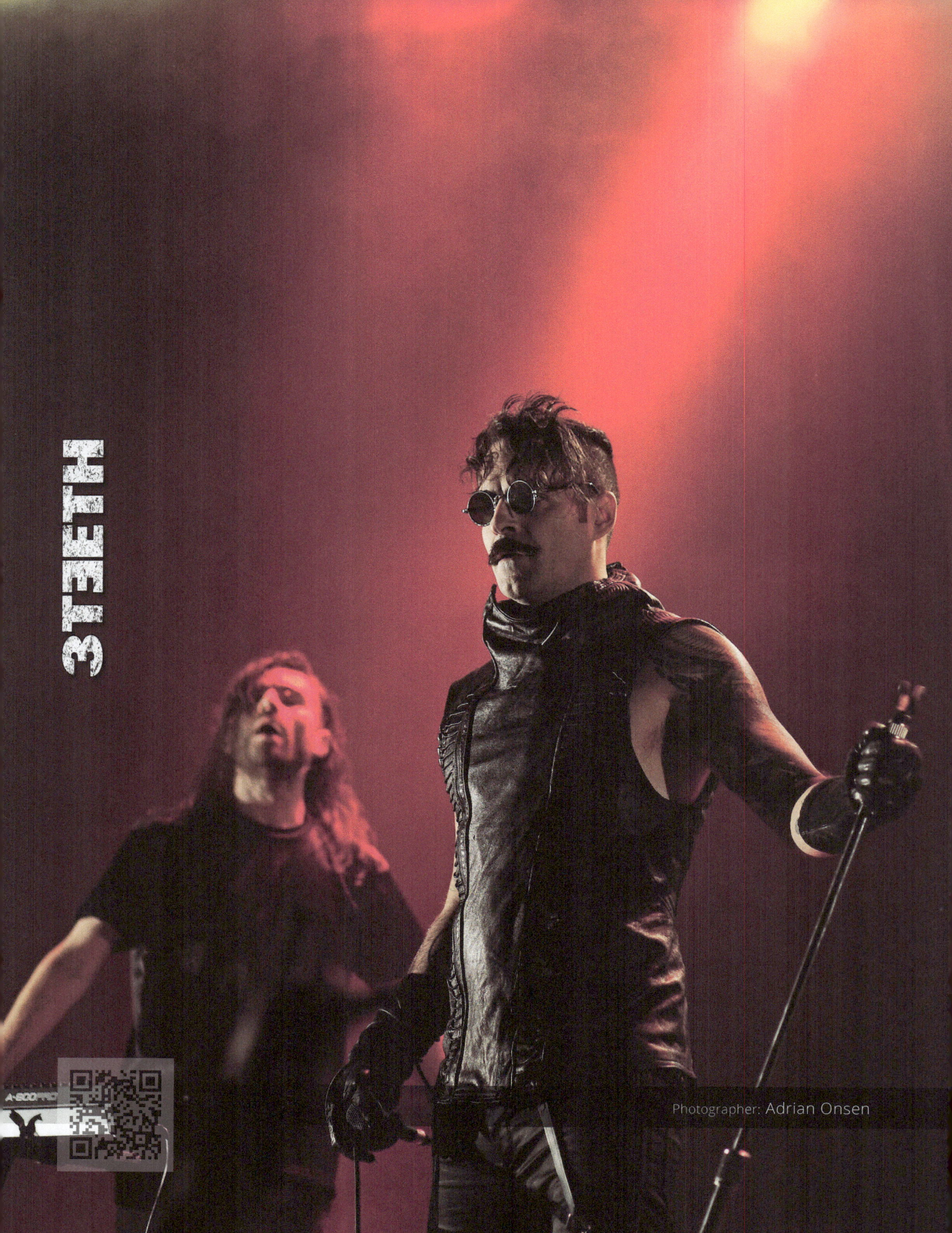

3TEETH

Photographer: Adrian Onsen

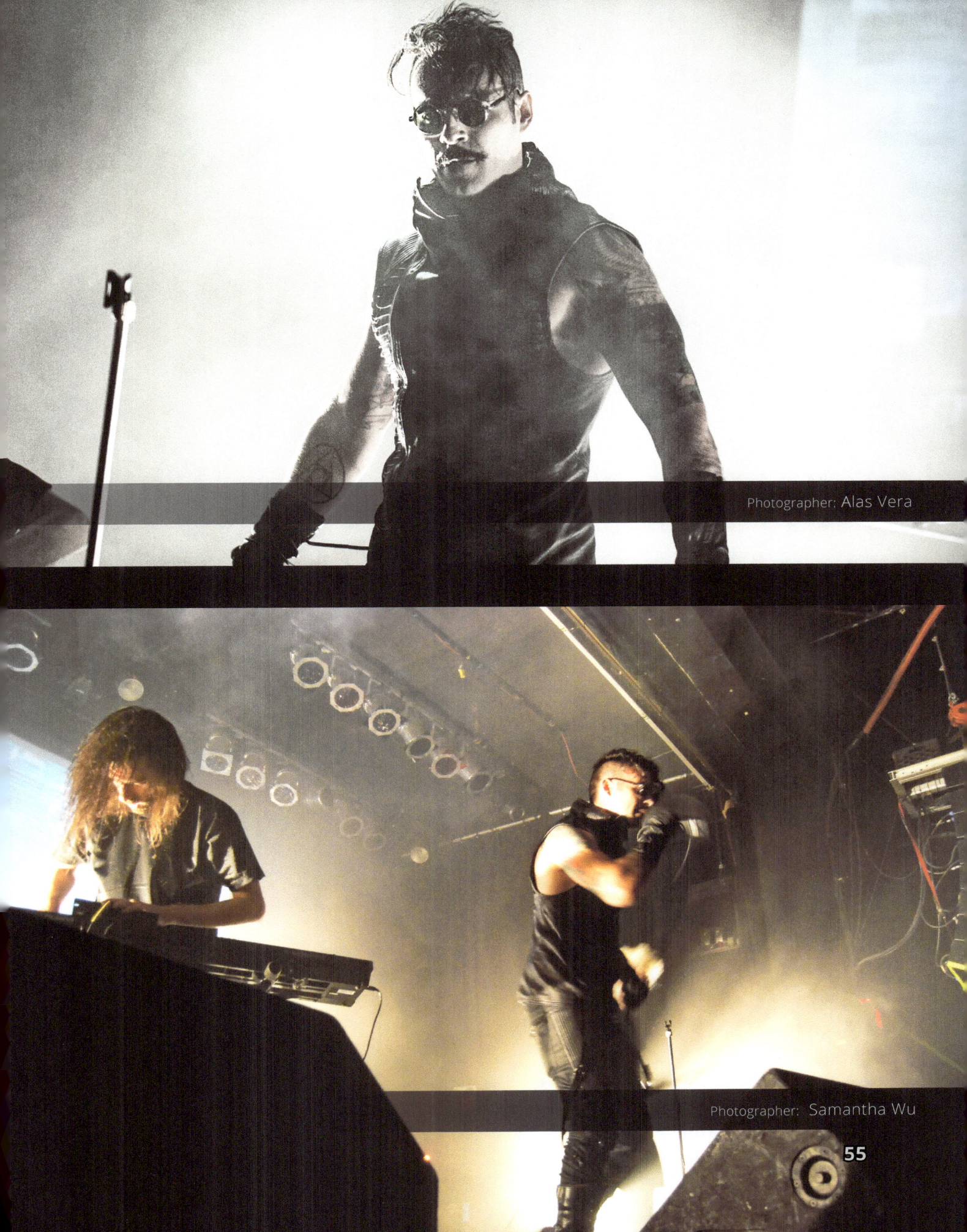

Photographer: Alas Vera

Photographer: Samantha Wu

conjure one

Photographer: Adrian Onsen

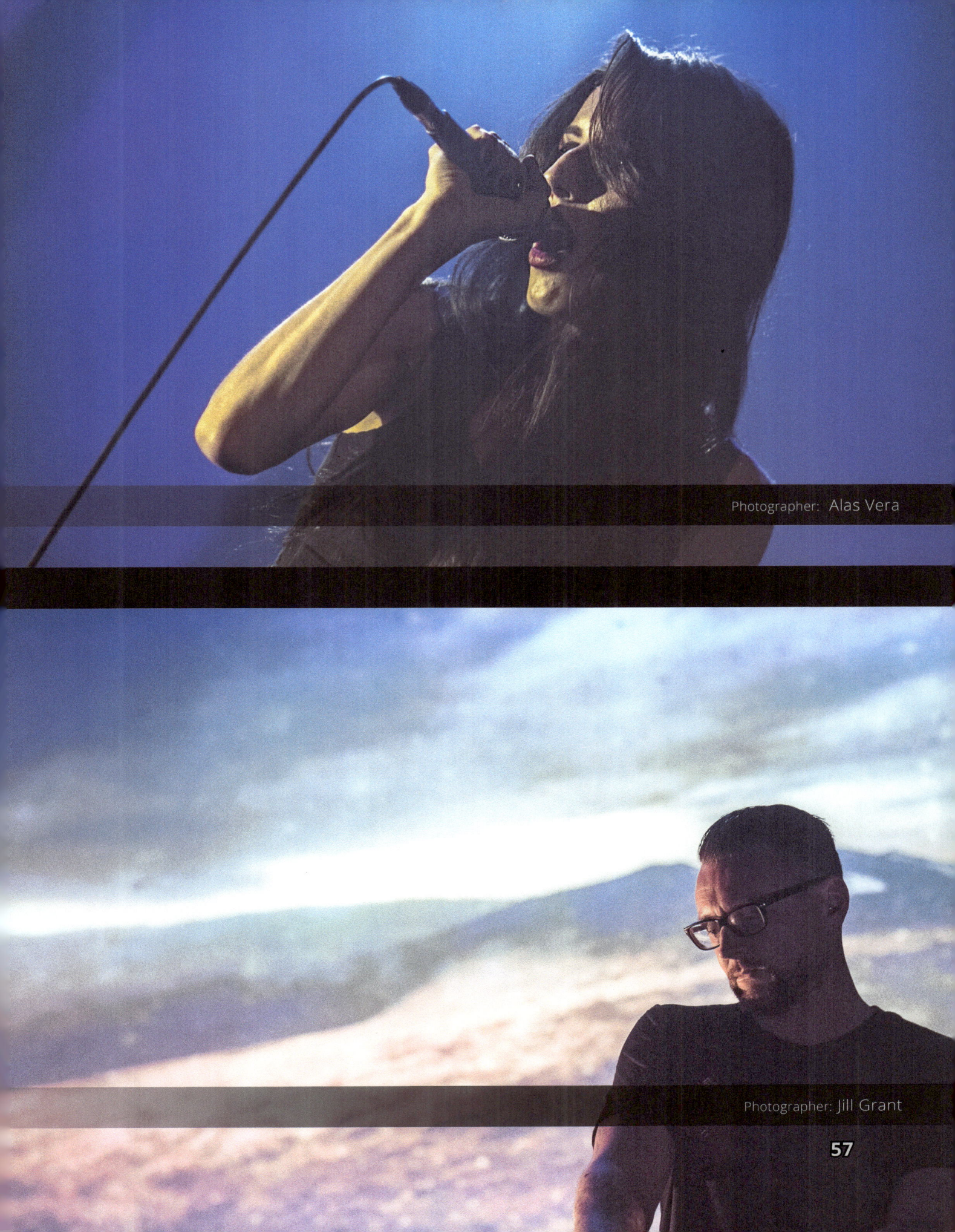

Photographer: Alas Vera

Photographer: Jill Grant

HAUJOBB

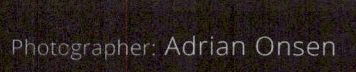

Photographer: Adrian Onsen

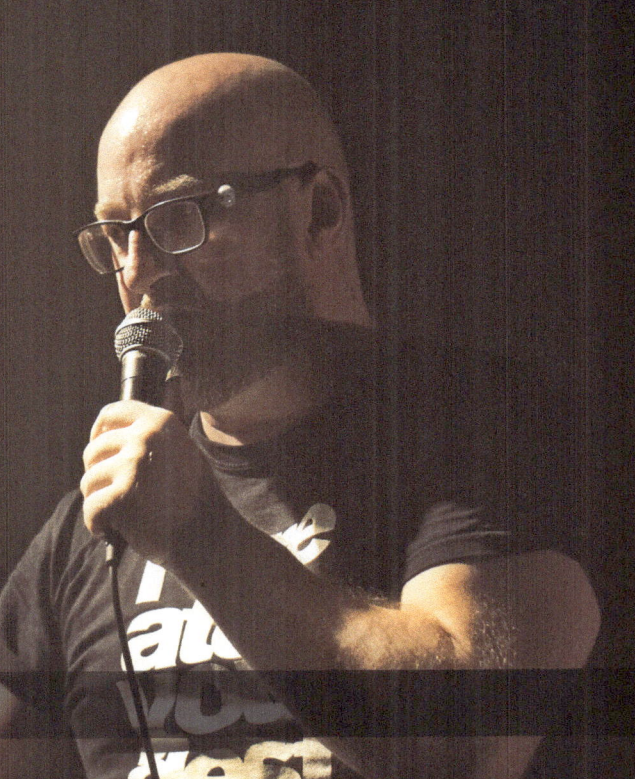

HAUJOBB

AFTERMATH

Since it's rare that we get booked for overseas festivals, we were both very excited that we got booked for Aftermath 2015. It was the only North American show we played in 2015 and the first time we played in Toronto. We have previously played 2 other Canadian shows, in Calgary and Montreal, and Canada has welcomed us with open arms every time we've played. We really do feel "home" in Canada. Aftermath was just amazing for us. We played an old-school set, as we always do when we play in a city for the first time. Most of the other bands are friends of ours so it was a bit like a class reunion, which always makes the bands perform with a pinch more humour, passion and dedication. We hope to return to Canada and Toronto soon again.

Hugs Claus & Kurt / Leæther Strip

I biked by the Phoenix a couple of times in the days following Aftermath.
I found myself suddenly missing the incredible energy of the festival.
After all the work, anticipation and worry, it all came together so wonderfully.

Glenn Love

For me, being involved with a festival right now, with this new band, Go Fight, is jarring. I never feel like we fit in very well. As an Electroscuzz band, we aren't really classically industrial. But Aftermath just felt really inclusive to us. It didn't matter what the individual bands were playing, the energy was so high, it felt right. The alarming thing to me about having to be a country western or pop musician, for example, would probably be the endless reminders that I didn't much connect with the people at the shows- other bands, people in the audience, etc. But there is a continuity of experience available here that is really impressive. There are so many cultural touchpoints to pull from, futurism, transhumanism, embracing technology, the optimism of a species moving forward, the political churn of a kind of individualized visceral rebellion. All of it seems to unify the people at festivals like this, creating a simple foundation to tell a story on. It's really exciting to be a part of it.

Jim Marcus / GoFight

Aftermath was a smooth running ship even when things went pear shaped. A Great crowd all excited about music, which is the Best environment to be in!
Not to mention the interest of a certain American label (NGP) which always puts wind the ol' sails.
Exciting weekend to say the least!

James Zirco Fisher / Squid Lid

Reflections on the Festival

For me, one of the great things about festivals like this is getting a chance to not just interact with bands that I love, but see them perform. I've been a fan of many of these bands for years, so whenever the chance comes up to see them, much less perform with them, we will always jump at it.
The crowd and venue also made Aftermath particularly memorable. I love the fact that shows that span the range of this scene are supported by everyone at the festival, new and old bands alike.
Thanks for having us!

Steven & Donna / Ego Likeness / Stoneburner

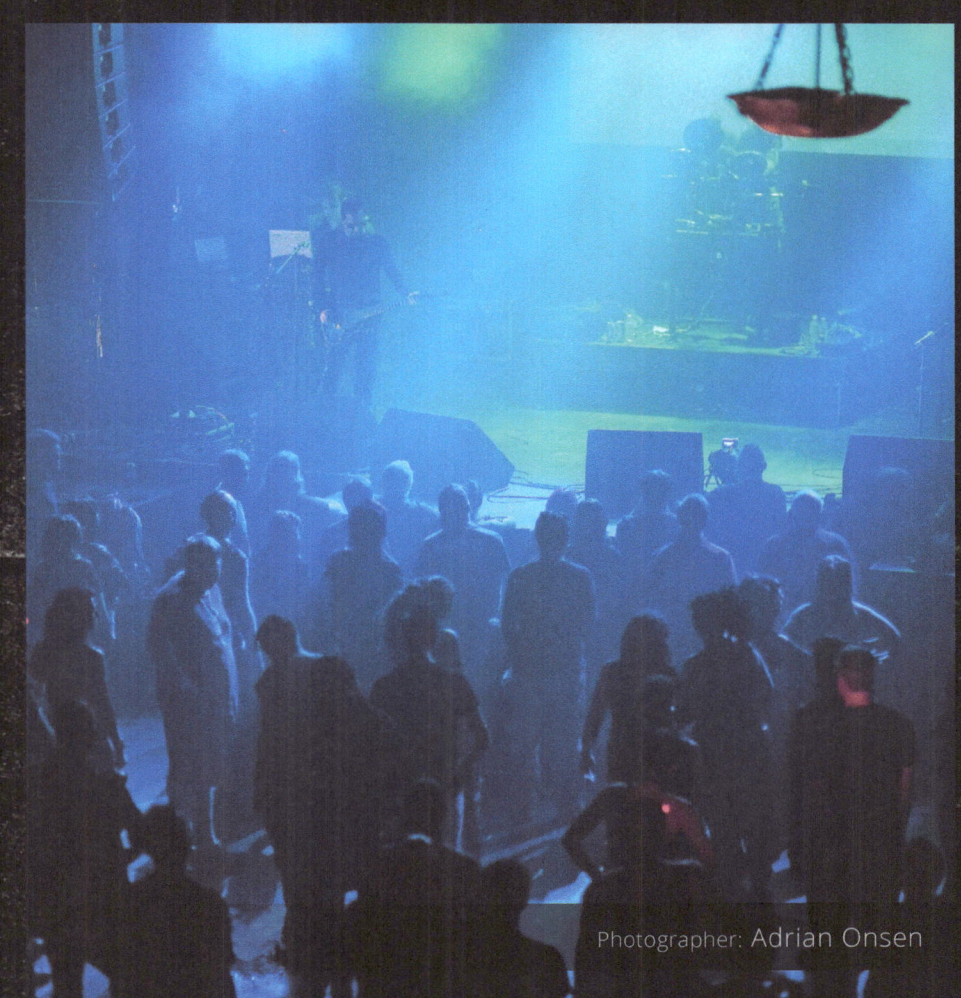

Photographer: Adrian Onsen

AFTERMATH

Being from Toronto, I didn't travel to see this festival. And when you're at home, it's much harder to resist the pull of the mundane and everyday. Much harder to get into the "festival" mood. But meeting those who did travel here and seeing Toronto through their eyes helped me realize how incredibly lucky we are. And it's a reminder that wonderful things happen in your own backyard if you're willing to get off your couch and experience them.

You also see how varied our subculture is and that we have a sort of family, no matter where we travel. It was very evident from those we met at Aftermath -- there was an instant connection, like long-lost relatives from another city. For example, the woman from St Louis who I had a (mostly drunken) conversation with in the washroom. She made me think about visiting the Midwest -- a region I would not have previously given much thought to seeing. So I'd say events like Aftermath are not only important for the music, they also widen our world and get us to discover our subculture in other cities.

Musically, there were a few highlights for me:

Mr.Kitty. New to me, but haunting synth pop that I can't seem to stop listening to.

The raw intensity of 3TEETH.

A stupendous and stompy set by Tactical Sekt that rocked my world.

The ethereal presence of Conjure One.

And if you stayed until the very end, specifically Haujobb, you were treated to an amazing show, with a couple of unique moments.

Daniel Myer reaching out his hand to a young woman in the crowd -- a Sistine Chapel kind of moment. In return he got a googly eye passed to him. (side note: upon returning home, we found the googly eyes stuck all over us. How did this happen? What could it mean?)

Mr.Kitty dancing on stage with Haujobb. Perfect juxtaposition of old and new that made me tear up a bit actually.

Daniel Myer singing "Everything Counts" at the end of his set. We all sang along with him, to a song recorded by Depeche Mode in 1984... I know some of us were actually around when that song was recorded and even if you weren't, it's a statement to the longevity of our subculture.

My humblest thanks to Troy Hilton for making this festival happen. I know the staggering amount of hard work that went into bringing us these moments. Until the next festival, googly eyes and all, here's looking at you Aftermath!!!

Beth Anderson

Reflections on the Festival

Aftermath, since its inception, has been a truly amazing thing. What I loved most about 2014's first edition was the overwhelming sense of pride and awe at what exactly this scene was capable of if it put its mind and heart into it. And that feeling definitely carried over into this year's festival - everybody I talked to was so happy to be there and to be a part of it. I think most people would agree that Aftermath is not just a music festival, but also a community. It felt like you couldn't go anywhere that weekend without meeting a new friend, or running into an old one, and everywhere I went I got into conversations or shenanigans with people from all over the place. A key part of this sense of community is also how laid back the bands are. It's not unusual to be browsing the merch table or waiting at the bar and realize one of the performers from the night before is beside you doing the same. They are all so approachable and seem to be having as much fun as the attendees – I trust by now we have all seen the video of Mr.Kitty teaching Daniel Myer and Ayria how to dance? This year hosted some tremendously talented bands, and I ate up every second of the performances. They gave the crowd everything they had, and I hope we gave it back just as intensely. I can't remember the last time I danced so much and so hard – the energy of the weekend was electric! On Sunday, closing the weekend out at the final night of Velvet Underground's existence was oddly fitting. While it was sad to say goodbye to a place so many of us had such fond memories in, it was impossible to feel anything but hopeful and excited about the future of our scene in Toronto and at large after a weekend like Aftermath brought us!

Stacey Masson

After the first year of Aftermath being put together in roughly 6 weeks and giving me a reason to have a renewed faith in the people in the scene, I can't deny having high expectations for the performers at the second year. Not one of them disappointed. Starting with the opening moments of the lights of Peter Turns Pirate and closing with the club night that was spread over two venues, Aftermath 2015 delivered on every level. Long time favorites like Velvet Acid Christ, Leæther Strip, and Kevorkian Death Cycle were just as impressive and enjoyable as 3TEETH, Squid Lid, and Mr.Kitty. All in all, one of the most enjoyable festivals I have ever had the fortune to attend.

Jonathan Wisniewski

AFTERMATH

Epilogue

I need to start by saying that I'm a fan of live music, not an artist, not a promoter, not a tech guy. Honestly, I know very little about music and the music industry. I came into this role, whatever it is, by simply going to shows and talking to people. Ten years ago I literally knew no one in the industry; now the vast majority of my friends are musicians, etc. I'm a registered nurse, and before nursing I worked with the Canadian military and as a guard in a maximum security jail. My background is people. I've made a career of observing behaviour and then intervening to alter outcome and mediate risk. It's from this standpoint that I became involved in Aftermath.

In 2014, when Kinetik fell apart, Troy Hilton (DSoL), Alex Kennedy and Bruce Lord (I Die: You Die), Scott Fox (iVardensphere) and Ryan & Alison Cameron-Clark (132 Productions) came together to and created something that had a strong feeling of community. I was very much a silent, back-line junior with this group, mostly helping with running around, liaison and the like, but I really liked the vibe that was created. This year, Troy approached me and asked me to work with him and Ben Vanlier (Ludovico Technique) to give it another go. From the beginning, this festival was a very different animal. Months of planning. All of the legwork involved in tracking down bands, deciding on lineups, negotiating fees, organizing flights and accommodations, and putting out fires, but through that, my goal was to try and retain that community feel. I firmly believe that there is a way of creating an event that is fair to the fans, artists, venues and all the other components that come together in these things, and I wanted to be the guy who helped find and massage that balance. I'm the guy who talks to people, hears their frustrations and then makes sure they have the best experience possible.

For the most part, I think we succeeded in the goal I set. I think those who travelled to Toronto and those who live here had a great time, seeing and doing things they maybe wouldn't have otherwise done. The artists and musicians all put on exceptional performances; for many this was their first time playing in either Toronto or Canada. I hope we opened both the fans and musicians up to something new. I DO know that there were several professional type conversations that came out of this festival, potentially creating touring, production, representation and other opportunities for several of the bands (I'm not allowed to let the cat out of the bag, but there were several bands who might see some benefits). Not only did we provide three full nights of excellent live music, but we also threw one hell of an after party. Our wake for Velvet Underground was fantastic, and when it was clear that Velvet was no more, we moved the party to Nocturne. This "little" move was the epitome of what I wanted for Aftermath. While I know there were those who grumbled about it, the management of two "rival" clubs worked together for the benefit of the scene. Members from bands who weren't on the bill came out to support their colleagues and promoters with competing interests pulled together and used their collective influence to solve problems. I think the transition from Velvet to Nocturne is the event that stands out in my mind as most important (Big thanks to Alison, Ryan and Spencer, Pat, Paul, Troy and Ritchie for your huge roles in this).

Sadly, because of administrative responsibilities I only heard, and didn't see, some of the bands I was most interested in. I'm grateful to Adrian for putting this book together. The pictures and stories it contains reflect a massive amount of hard work from a great many people, most of them friends.

Richard Trotter

AFTERMATH

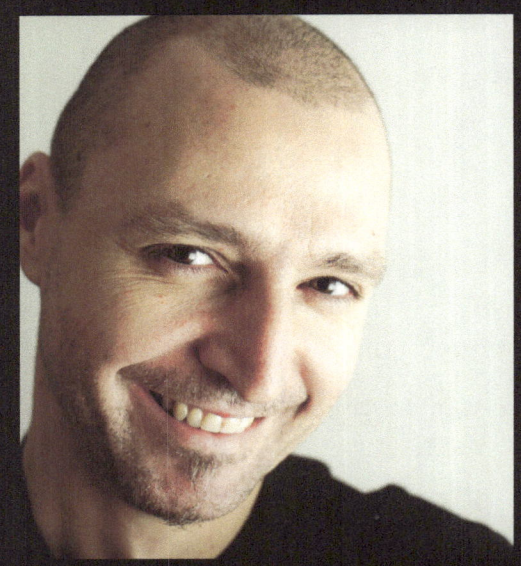

From a love of music and photography, the passion to capture artists at their peak performance was born.

The moments of expression when the perfromer is in their game, giving it their craft everything they have in a way that only they can, are often very brief moments. Those special snapshots in time are what Adrian Onsen currently strives to capture.

Traveling locally and abroad to find exceptional music and exceptional artists is where he's at these days. Follow him on FB at Onsendesigns Photography or website at:

photo.onsendesigns.com

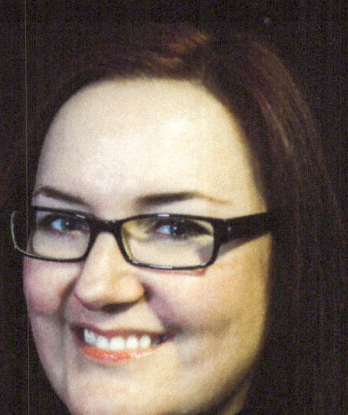

Music fan and hobby photographer, Jill Grant is happiest when the two worlds intersect. As a result, you can find her and her camera all over Toronto and beyond chasing down photographs of great live music. She has contributed images to a variety of projects including her concert photography blog at :

takeitforgranted.ca

Contributing Photographers

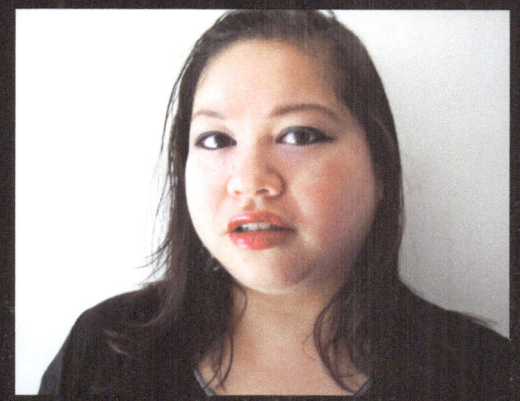

Samantha loves to write and she loves the arts. She also loves combining the two. She's a senior photojournalist for Lithium Magazine (ww.lithiummagazine.com), editor/writer for Mooney on Theatre (www.mooneyontheatre.com), and copy editor/writer for Art Katalyst magazine (www.artkatalyst.com). She's passionate about music, theatre, photography, writing, and celebrating sexuality - not necessarily in that order. She drinks tea more than coffee, prefers ciders over beers, and sings karaoke way too loudly. You can find her on all major social media (Facebook, Twitter and Instagram) at: **@says_samanthawu.**

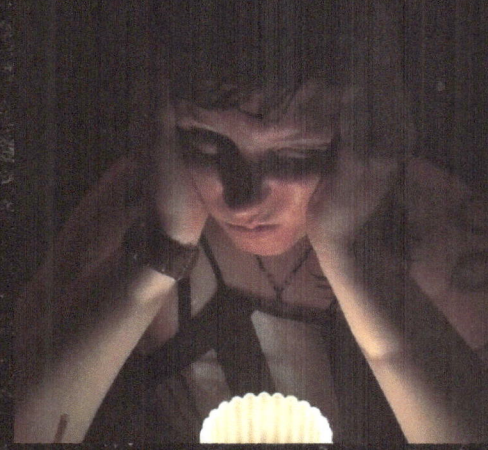

Being a nomadic traveler Alas Vera still gets out to photograph from time to time.
Visit her youtube channel:
www.youtube.com/user/Zinthra/videos

www.ingramcontent.com/pod-product-compliance
Lightning Source LLC
Chambersburg PA
CBHW051044180526
45172CB00002B/512